Somewhere near the center of Wallace Stevens' poetic vision are delight—the hedonist's delight in the thoughts and feelings, the things and sounds and colors which comprise the goods of this world—and the poet's ambition to make this delight accessible to others. This book examines Stevens' literary career —particularly the poems of the *Harmonium* period—with a special eye to the hazards risked by a modern American artist who takes his delight seriously.

That among these hazards is a sense of oneself as "A most inappropriate man/ In a most unpropitious place" is perhaps inevitable. Herbert J. Stern provides a fresh perspective on Stevens' comic spirit, showing that the comic element in his work frequently takes the form of self-mockery. Stern also argues that Stevens' passion for philosophical and aesthetic speculation was an essential element of his poetry from the beginning. And running through Stern's discussions of the individual poems is a basic underlying premise: that the excellence of Stevens' poetry issued from his ability to set opposing aspects of his mind against one another and to distil from these confrontations an art whose vitality is in its own self-questioning.

Wallace Stevens
Art of Uncertainty

Wallace Stevens

Art of Uncertainty

———

by
Herbert J. Stern

Ann Arbor
The University of Michigan Press

Grateful acknowledgment is made for permission to
quote from the following:

ALFRED A. KNOPF, INC.

Collected Poems by Wallace Stevens, copyright 1923, 1931, 1935,
1936, 1937, 1942, 1943, 1944, 1945, 1946, 1947, 1948
1949, 1950, 1951, 1952, 1954 by Wallace Stevens.

The Necessary Angel by Wallace Stevens, copyright 1942, 1944,
1947, 1948, 1949, 1951 by Wallace Stevens.

Opus Posthumous by Wallace Stevens, copyright © 1957 by
Elsie Stevens and Holly Stevens.

Letters of Wallace Stevens, edited by Holly Stevens,
copyright © 1966 by Holly Stevens.

HOUGHTON MIFFLIN COMPANY

A Critical Fable by Amy Lowell, copyright © 1922
by Houghton Mifflin Company.

THE MACMILLAN COMPANY, MACMILLAN & CO., LTD., AND
MR. M. B. YEATS

The Collected Poems of W. B. Yeats,
copyright © 1940 by Georgie Yeats.

For Andrée and for Irvin

Preface

My PRINCIPAL AIM in this study is threefold. I wish to establish, first, that Wallace Stevens' passion for philosophical and aesthetic speculation, far from representing a late and, in the view of many of his critics, unfortunate development in his literary career, was in fact an inherent, even essential, aspect of his poetry from the beginning. By entering into the world of his first book, *Harmonium,* through the portals of his subsequent essays on poetic theory, I have sought to demonstrate that for Stevens poetry had always served the function of testing aesthetic, epistemological and other more broadly philosophical premises. Second, for the better part of the decade following the publication of *Harmonium,* Stevens abandoned the poetic art over which he had already achieved mastery; in doing this, as I have tried to show, he was responding not only to the exigent demands of his career as insurance executive, but also to forces within his own art which for the time being denied the possibility of art itself. My third aim is to demonstrate that Stevens as hedonist and Stevens as humanist, Stevens as witty skeptic and Stevens as romantic meliorist, though they spoke with various voices, indeed were one. Somewhere near the center of Stevens' aesthetic and his humanism is delight—the hedonist's delight in the thoughts and feelings, the things and sounds and colors which comprise the goods of this world; and the poetic meliorist's ambition to make this delight accessible to others, to make his imagination the imagination of his auditors.

The methods of my critical approach, although they range eclectically through biographical, aesthetic, and textual commentary, are informed by a common general premise—that the excellence of Stevens' art issued from his ability to cast opposing aspects of his mind against one another, and to distil from these internal struggles a poetry whose vitality is in its own self-questioning.

In establishing this thesis, I have traced the dualities that are evident in the critical approaches to Stevens' work, in his sometimes uneasily yoked careers of insurance executive and poet, and in the poetry of the *Harmonium* period itself. I have made use, insofar as the limits of my topic could permit, of the total body of his published work, some of it not available before the appearance of *Opus Posthumous* in 1957. Inevitably, I have also drawn much, directly and indirectly, from other students of Stevens' writings. And finally, my own confidence in my premises has been immeasurably enhanced by my study of unpublished letters and manuscripts which the generosity of university libraries and of scholars has made available to me.

It is my hope that by utilizing these techniques in my examination of these materials, I have been able to establish that for Stevens the poetic testing of what his profession calls surety claims comprised a quest for the certainties left to us in a skeptical age, and foreshadows an early conviction of a truth he expressed late: that

> the relation of art to life is of first importance especially in a skeptical age since, in the absence of a belief in God, the mind turns to its own creations and examines them, not alone from the aesthetic point of view, but for what they validate and invalidate, for the support that they give.

Although the intellectual debts and the debts of human generosity I have accrued during the writing of this study cannot be repaid here, they can be acknowledged. To the officers of Wabash College, and particularly to Deans Benjamin A. Rogge and Norman C. Moore, my gratitude for their unwavering moral support and for the several grants that made my research possible. My thanks also to my colleagues Owen Duston and Karl O'Lessker, and to Mrs. Dolores Maxwell, for reading sections of this study, and for encouragement and suggestions that improved it. To my friends Lysander Kemp and Morris Beja I am grateful for reading the manuscript in its entirety, and for helping me to smooth at least some of its rough edges. And to my friend Charles Blinderman my thanks for his help in getting the manuscript through the final stages of preparation. I owe much to Samuel French Morse and Michel Benamou for their generous response to my queries, and for information that first led me toward Stevens' unpublished letters. I am equally indebted to the late R. P. Blackmur and to Northrup Frye for suggestions and assistance that set me on rewarding trails. Conrad Aiken, Stanley Burnshaw, John Dos Passos, and Carl Van Vechten were gracious in responding to my requests for reminiscences and facts. I wish to thank also Robert Rosenthal, curator of manuscripts, and Mrs. Judith

Bond, former curator of the Harriet Monroe Modern Poetry Collection, both of the University of Chicago; Miss Doris M. Reed, curator of manuscripts at the Lilly Library, Indiana University; and William H. Bond, curator of manuscripts at the Houghton Library, Harvard University. My special thanks are due Miss Agnes Elpers and Professor Philip B. Daghlian of the Indiana University Department of English for acts of kindness which helped make the completion of this study possible; and to Mrs. Winifred Wertz for her skill in typing the manuscript.

Since the original version of my manuscript was completed, Mr. Donald Hall's interest and concrete encouragement have been of immeasurable help and comfort to me. And Miss Holly Stevens, to whom I am also grateful for permission to quote from her father's letters, has given of her time, her knowledge, and her hospitality with an openhandedness for which my thanks here are small thanks indeed.

The man to whose patience, friendship, and excellence of mind I feel most obligated has preferred to remain nameless here. Finally, to my wife, Andrée, I am grateful for all the reasons in the world.

Contents

I

Children Picking up Our Bones

ONE BEGINS A JOURNEY like Laertes, burdened with injunctions, and it is probably well that the critic who prepares to enter the looking-glass world of Wallace Stevens pay special regard to the warning André Gide issued to those who would reassemble the bones he left behind: "My children, I pray that you do not understand me too quickly." Stevens, too, some twenty years before he died, had thoughts on his children:

> Children picking up our bones
> Will never know that these were once
> As quick as foxes on the hill; . . .
>
>   Children,
> Still weaving budded aureoles,
> Will speak our speech and never know,
>
> Will say of the mansion that it seems
> As if he that lived there left behind
> A spirit storming in blank walls,
>
> A dirty house in a gutted world,
> A tatter of shadows peaked to white,
> Smeared with the gold of the opulent sun.[1]

It is the way with children to understand too quickly or not at all, and the critical children of Stevens' poetry have at times been guilty both of the sin of commission and omission.

For the moment, however, it is with the temptation to understand too quickly that we are concerned. Two separate lures may attract us in this direction, and they are lures doubly deadly because when they are offered by other poets they conceal nothing baleful. The first of these lures entices us to read Stevens' poems singly, and to attempt, in the recent critical fashion, to understand the poet's intention simply by understanding what is there on the page. Examples of this technique appear almost monthly in such periodicals as *The Explicator,* and with few exceptions, they offer painful object lessons in the danger I have described.[2] Even so perceptive, if at times perverse, a critic as Yvor Winters has been guilty of reading individual poems out of their context (a context composed, to the critic's despair, of everything Stevens has written), and in so doing he has been forced to conclude that "The Mechanical Optimist"[3] is an example of "laborious foolishness," and "Earthy Anecdote," of "some of [Stevens'] most willful nonsense."[4]

If we are to avoid the error of Winters and others, and if we are to understand (slowly) Stevens' unique gifts, we must first be aware that the body of his work is a kind of monadology in which each poem not only reflects special aspects of each other poem but also illuminates the whole of Stevens' cosmos from a particular area of perception. Primary authority for such a view must come, of course, from a familiarity with Stevens' entire *oeuvre;* more specific evidence, however, may be discovered in Stevens' "conviction that all his books would eventually make one book, 'The Whole of Harmonium,' as he first wanted to call the *Collected Poems*,"[5] and in the suggestion he once made to Alfred A. Knopf that the book later published as *Harmonium* be called "The Grand Poem: Preliminary Minutiae."[6]

There can in fact be little question that Stevens conceived of his poems as parts of a whole, or that the completed body of his work is, depending on one's point of view, either far more coherent or far more repetitious in theme than that of any other modern poet with the possible exception of Yeats. Neither can we assume that this notion of general coherence was a late development in Stevens' thought, for in 1917 or 1918 he wrote to William Carlos Williams:

> My idea is that in order to carry a thing to the extreme [necessary] to convey it one has to stick to it. . . . Given a fixed point of view, realistic, imagistic, or what you will, everything adjusts to that point of view; and the process of adjustment is a world in flux, as it should always be for a poet. But to fidget with points of view leads always to new beginnings and incessant new beginnings lead to sterility. A single manner or mode thoroughly mature and exploited is that fresh thing.[7]

The ideal approach to any of Stevens' poems, then, is by tracing its correspondences with everything else Stevens wrote, and, thereby, with that single manner or mode of which it is part. Granted the practical impossibility of this critical method, it will nevertheless be well to keep it before us as an ideal.

The second of the lures to which I referred earlier once more concerns the question of context. Particularly in the recent past, when, with the publication of *The Necessary Angel* in 1951, Stevens' critical essays became generally available, it has been fashionable to extract individual statements made in the essays and to offer them as Stevens' final thoughts on whatever subject may be in question. Louis Martz is guilty of such an error when, in an attempt to prove that *Ideas of Order* is in fact what Stevens wished it to be, a "Farewell to Florida" and to the southern vision that dominated *Harmonium*, he quotes Stevens' own critical statement that "the poet must get rid of the hieratic in everything that concerns him" and that he must abolish "the false conception of the imagination as some incalcuable *vates* within us, unhappy Rodomantade."[8] In addition to the fact that the second statement was severed from a context that renders it highly ambiguous, it is important, also, to insist that for Stevens such abolition could never be a *fait accompli* but was rather a continuous dialectical struggle.

Whatever it is that the poet *must* do, Stevens was no better able to legislate against himself than critics have been able to do for him. It may be that for every dogmatic statement Stevens has made in prose, a contradictory statement can be found elsewhere in his writing. The series of aphorisms published after his death as "Adagia" offers dramatic illustrations of this truth. For example:

> What we see in the mind is as real to us as what we see by the eye.

> There is nothing in life except what one thinks of it.

> Poetry has to be something more than a conception of the mind. It has to be a revelation of nature. Conceptions are artificial. Perceptions are essential.

> The poem is a nature created by the poet.

4

The ultimate value is reality.

Reality is a vacuum.

Eventually an imaginary world is entirely without interest.[9]

What is striking here is the fact that Stevens' mind was spacious and hospitable enough to entertain such antagonistic guests without apparent strain, or, at least, without strain apparent to those who have formulated consistent theories of the imagination on the basis of his work. Lest the critic be guilty of carving a procrustean order at the sacrifice of vital antinomies, he should be aware that Stevens' rage for order, like Donne's, was matched only by his delight in paradox ("a law of inherent opposites,/ Of essential unity, is as pleasant as port," as he put it in "Connoisseur of Chaos"[10]), and we will only lose the vitality of that unity if we ignore the inherent opposites which it comprises.

An examination of the general patterns of critical response which Stevens' work has inspired will suggest that the average critic's mind, like the poet's, contains housemaid as well as sloven, insatiable shaper as well as "connoisseur of chaos," student of the "essential unity" as well as another diligent to pursue the "law of inherent opposites." The importance of such an examination will be in establishing a concept central to this study: that there exists in Stevens' work a gradual movement in emphasis, from a commitment to the imagination *in vacuo* to a balancing concern with reality, or what Stevens is fond of calling "things as they are." In the course of this examination we shall discover a fact more surprising than it appears: that critical opinion of Stevens has shifted from a concern with his aestheticism to fascination with his humanism, from an interest in

5

what he has termed the "hieratic" quality of his poetry to what he again has called the "credible."[11] What makes such critical dogging less in the nature of things than one might expect is that the poetic movement described is not a change from one view to another—not, to put it differently, a case of poetic development in the conventional sense—but rather a slow inclination from one pole to another, *both* poles having already been firmly established by 1923, the year which, with the publication of *Harmonium*, marks the end of Stevens' first period.

The dominant impression made on the contemporary readers of the work of this early period might well be summed up with the single word "preciosity." This is not to say that critics were unimpressed by the solid mastery of Stevens' style, or even that there were not several who perceived and to an extent illuminated Stevens' ideas on the relations between reality and the imagination. What is true, however, is that the early reviewers and critics were almost universal in their preoccupation with the sensuousness of music and imagery, the delicacy, even the finickiness, of the shaping imagination. Few of them shared the perceptiveness of Marianne Moore, when, in 1924, she wrote, "The author's violence is for aggrandizement, not for stupor,"[12] and even Miss Moore, in what is certainly the most brilliant of these early reviews, was more concerned with the "love of magnificence" and "the riot of gorgeousness in which Mr. Stevens' imagination takes refuge" than in the nature of the aggrandizement.[13]

Speaking generally, the exotic scenes against which so many of Stevens' early imaginative promenades take place, the Keatsian lushness of rhythm and diction to be found in such poems as "Sunday Morning" or "Le Monocle de Mon Oncle," the curiously ironic euphuism of "The Comedian as the Letter C," with titles as delectable and apparently as mystifying as the poems that followed them, had for even the more sympathetic early readers the fascination which a dark odalisque from a decadent romance might have for a Hawthorne-like Puritan. For those of more resolutely austere stomachs, perusal of the early poems frequently seemed a cloying experience, an exposure to textures too dense, tapestry figures too baroquely stylized, words too savoringly mouthed, and attitudes too delicately assumed.

Thus George Soule, who in 1916 offered what appears to be the earliest critical notice of Stevens' work, could concede no more than that "the delicate and fantastic 'Peter Quince at the Clavier' . . . has at least momentary charm."[14] Max Michelson, writing two years later in the same languid and grudging vein, observed:

> Wallace Stevens' group has charm, but it is somewhat romantic. I mean the charm is due to a romantic sort of exaggeration. It is not unlike the Georgian Anthology; though modernized. Or, it is tired Chinese—if that has any meaning to you—which the mood cannot condone.[15]

Less tentative critics were before long giving more cogent and responsible expression to similar observations. Reviewing *Harmonium* in 1923, John Gould Fletcher sought to account for Stevens' fastidious aestheticism by remarking that "he is out of tune with life and with his surroundings, and is seeking to escape into a sphere of finer harmony between instinct and intelligence."[16] Although Fletcher was unsympathetic with what he saw as a general movement toward "aestheticism and premature senility" in American poetry, he considered Stevens " at all events an honest aesthete," and one whose aestheticism was supported by "the finest and most distinguished weapon of style."[17] Even Stevens' obscurity, Fletcher argues, unlike what he found in *The Waste Land*, "the best work of the Sitwells," or even Paul Valéry's "Jeune Parque," "comes from a wealth of meaning and allusion which are unavoidable; and his intention, when we finally fathom it, is far clearer and more earnestly pursued than theirs."[18]

Llewelyn Powys, although somewhat disturbed by a "bizarre, niggling sensuality in accord with some dainty physical disability" which seemed to him latent in *Harmonium*,[19] nevertheless moved still closer to defining the particular genus of Stevens' aestheticism when he wrote:

> It may well be that his eccentric verse does reveal more of the insecure, fluctuating secrets of the universe than are to be found in other, more sedate, more decorous artistic creations. Wavering, uncertain, bereft of ancient consolation, the human race comes more and more to realize that it has won to consciousness in a world which is relative and undulating. In such a world it is indeed impossible that intimations of some incalculable absolute are more nearly to be come at under the influence of cloud shadows floating beneath a violet moon than under that of the splashes of actual sunshine lying so confidently on grass, and brick, and metal.[20]

Powys was aware, however tentatively, of a fact that Yvor Winters later proved incapable of recognizing: that for Stevens the modern poem was

> *The poem of the mind in the act of finding*
> *What will suffice. It has not always had*
> *To find: the scene was set; it repeated what*
> *Was in the script.*

Children Picking Up Our Bones

Then the theatre was changed
To something else. Its past was a souvenir.[21]

Yet in spite of this tentative awareness of the philosophical background for Stevens' aestheticism, Powy's central contention was that Stevens had erected a Palace of Art which, however exquisite, was at the same time obsessively morbid and strange.

It is again the escapist theme that troubled Gorham B. Munson in 1925. Less sympathetic than Powys with cloud shadows, Munson complained of Stevens' reluctance to grapple with the horror and misery of the world. In Stevens' passion for detached tranquility, Munson saw a reflection of a quality characteristically American—the obsession with material comfort. "Is there not fundamentally a kinship between the sensory discriminations and comfortable tranquillity of Wallace Stevens' poetry and the Americans that own baronial estates?"[22] Munson asked, with perhaps more regard for passion than coherence. Like Powys, Munson was aware of Stevens' rage for order, but whereas Powys, almost against his will, was fascinated by Stevens' Palace of Art, Munson was indignant with it; he viewed Stevens as an escapist who, through the imagination, invented a literary cosmos which is "whole and understandable, and therefore a refuge in life that is fragmentary and perplexing. It, in being form, is a polite answer to the hugeness which we cannot form."[23]

It would be neither wise nor gracious to dismiss out of hand these early judgments of Stevens' work. Indeed, what may seem most remarkable to the modern reader is that a volume which sold fewer than a hundred copies should have attracted the responsible critical attention devoted to *Harmonium*. It is also true that several of these early reviews must have touched raw nerves which were already giving Stevens pain. How disturbing it must have been for him, at the very moment before he abandoned his poetry for six years, to read Fletcher's apposite warning: "But for the future he must face a clear choice of evils: he must either expand his range to take in more of human experience, or give up writing altogether. 'Harmonium' is a sublimation which does not permit of a sequel."[24] And was it, one wonders, with an air of self-vindication that in 1935, when the sequel did in fact appear, Stevens wore the robe of the Lady of Shalott, floating down to the Camelot of human experience?

It is in any case certain that the charge against the cloistered quality of Stevens' art, particularly during the *Harmonium* period, was an accurate one, however limited were the perceptions on which it was usually based. Where Stevens would have differed with his detractors is over the moral judgment implied by the term "escapism." He would no doubt have argued in 1923, as he later did in 1942, that the poetic process

> is psychologically an escapist process. . . . My own remarks about resisting or evading the pressure of reality mean escapism, if analyzed. Escapism has a perjorative sense, which it cannot be supposed that I include in the sense in which I use the word. The pejorative sense applies where the poet is not attached to reality, where the imagination does not adhere to reality, which, for my part, I regard as fundamental.[25]

Very well, we can imagine Munson, for example, replying; but having granted the necessity of this attachment, what social obligations do you ascribe to the poet? The poet's role, argued Stevens in the essay from which I have just quoted, "is to help people to live their lives.

He has had immensely to do with giving life whatever savor it possesses."[26] Providing such savor, however, is not a social obligation but purely an aesthetic one. Whereas Stevens' detractors have complained of his failure to perform the classical task of holding a mirror up to nature, Stevens himself has conceived the poet's task, in an age when reality has become violent,[27] to be the reconstruction of a nature worthy of holding a mirror up to. "The author's violence," as Marianne Moore perceived, "is for aggrandizement, not for stupor."

Critics like Fletcher, Powys, Munson, and Marianne Moore performed invaluable service to Stevens' art by examining it seriously at a time when few were willing to examine it at all. Through their frequently narrow understanding of the motives for Stevens' dandyism and aestheticism, however, they provided the threads for what is perhaps the most serious misinterpretation into which Stevens' work has been entangled: the tendency of most American critics and reviewers until about 1940, and of their English counterparts until quite recently, to see Stevens as Yeats saw Keats, in the figure of a schoolboy "with face and nose pressed to a sweet shop window." This view was recently examined by Frank Kermode, in one of the few knowledgeable studies of Stevens to appear in an English journal. In Kermode's view, the two main difficulties "responsible for our English reluctance to accept Wallace Stevens as a major poet" are, first, "his notorious gaudiness," and second, "the common assumption that Stevens is a very narrow poet, having poetry, and almost nothing else, as his subject."[28]

The second and more complex of these difficulties we have already touched on indirectly; for the moment we need only add that for Stevens, to have poetry, and almost nothing else, for one's subject is precisely equivalent to having everything, and almost nothing else, for one's subject. That, in effect, is what he argued, with somewhat faulty logic, in 1947 when he wrote:

> It comes to this, that poetry is a part of the structure of reality. If this has been demonstrated, it pretty much amounts to saying that the structure of poetry and the structure of reality are one, or should be.[29]

The first difficulty, as Mr. Kermode is aware, should have been allayed once and for all by an essay written by R. P. Blackmur in 1931, the year when interest in Stevens had grown sufficiently to encourage Knopf to publish a second edition of *Harmonium*. The great virtue of Blackmur's essay was that it ignored questions concerning the social responsibility of the poet in favor of those related to Stevens' diction. As Kermode suggests, the euphuistic gaudiness of Stevens' language is one of the qualities which may encourage readers to consider his poetry primarily decorative, and therefore minor. But Blackmur demonstrates apodictically that "Good poets gain their excellency by writing an existing language *as if* it were their own invention," and that Stevens, "by combining the insides of those words he found fit to his feelings" (unlike E. E. Cummings, who "succeeded mainly in turning his words into empty shells") was able to "turn his words into knowledge."[30] It is true that Blackmur failed to observe that Stevens is capable of a deliberate gaudiness, as in "The Comedian as the Letter C," where he employs a consistently euphuistic diction as an instrument of self-parody, and it is also true that in discussing "Disillusionment of Ten O'Clock" Blackmur confused ironically extravagant metaphor with what he considers an "actual entrance into nonsense";[31] but for all that, this early essay is as indispensable today as it was more than three decades ago to those who would understand Stevens' "notorious gaudiness" as one of his devices of aggrandizement.

With the publication of *Ideas of Order* in 1935, questions of escapism and social responsibility were raised once more, this time by leftist critics. Stanley Burnshaw, writing in *New Masses,* saw the earlier work of Stevens as the kind "that people concerned with the murderous world collapse can hardly swallow today except in tiny doses."[32] *Ideas of Order,* on the other hand, although clearly related to the new political realities, was for Burnshaw the strangely confused "record of a man who, having lost his footing, scrambles to stand up and keep his balance."[33] It is not, perhaps, any more remarkable that a poet like Stevens, for whom "the structure of poetry and the structure of reality are one, or should be," should have lost his footing under the impact of the violently unpoetic Thirties than that Yeats, some fifteen years earlier, should similarly have tottered before the social and military upheavals of his time. The best poets of our era have been precarious equilibrists. However, it is interesting to observe that whereas a decade earlier the critics were troubled by Stevens' reluctance to emerge from the Ivory Tower, the tendency of the new generation of the Thirties was to express dissatisfaction over Stevens' failure, once having emerged, to set their world immediately to rights. Although Stevens himself was to observe during this same period, that "a great disorder is an order,"[34] his critics have at times been less than gracious in demanding of him in a period of violent upheaval the same lapidary verse that they had complained against earlier, in times of peace.

That *Ideas of Order* did in fact reflect the confusion of the times that engendered it has never been seriously doubted. Hi Simons, writing apolitically in 1940, agreed with Burnshaw in regarding the volume as

> above all a response to the disorder in society and in ideas that was current at the time. The sense of bewildered alarm over approaching disintegration which it evinces—its raising of questions for which only tentative answers are given—is the characterizing aspect of Stevens' work during this period.[35]

Yet, even while Stevens' poetry became preoccupied with disorder, his reputation was for the first time beginning to appear solid and established. Simons could conclude his study of the vicissitudes of Stevens' critical reputation with the confident statement that "however the future may evaluate [Stevens'] contributions to that small body of certain poetry which represents our times, his contemporaries have accepted it as great,"[36] and his confidence was justified by the fact that he was able to express it in a special "Wallace Stevens Number" of *The Harvard Advocate*. It was not, however, simply the existence of this tribute which constituted its importance. The issue contained, in addition to Simons' essay, articles or brief comments by F. O. Matthiessen, Marianne Moore, Allen Tate, William Carlos Williams, and others. It is true that Williams heaved a small apple of discord into the generally festive company by writing: "Stevens is a far better poet than his critical standards seem to indicate. May his will decay as he ages and his daemon get more and more the upper hand."[37] Williams' restrained dissatisfaction, however, was largely drowned out by the enthusiasm of his fellows, and the enthusiasm was shored up by a variety of keen critical judgments.

Certainly the most original, and probably the most valuable, of *The Harvard Advocate* essays was John

Finch's "North and South in Stevens' America." Taking sharp issue with earlier commentators on *Harmonium*, Finch demonstrated that

> Those who found Harmonium gorgeous and dreamy and nothing more, those to whom Oklahoma, Tallapoosa, and Tehuantepec sounded as remote as Xanadu, Auber, and Weir, were reading only a surface and misreading that.[38]

For Stevens, Finch went on, these place names are not manifestations of exoticism but are rather one of the devices by which Stevens sought to define and evaluate "his soil and his society."[39] Finch was sensitive to Stevens' passionate allegiance to the tropic warmth and sensuality of the imagination's southern pole, symbol of the exotic, the romantic, and fit complement to the insatiably fecund imagination; he was also aware, however, that Stevens' South is, significantly, "without spring—it is a place that does not nourish."[40] The North, on the other hand, although frigid and polar, is a place to which spring comes. Precisely because it denies and contradicts the imagination, it is capable also of nourishing it through opposition, and of offering a higher freedom and more significant order than are possible in the lotus lands of the South. Finch was here drawing significant new lines of approach to Stevens' poetry; and if his short essay is deficient in any respect it is in his failure to discover the seeds of the conflict between North and South already evident in *Harmonium*.

    A view similar to Finch's, although advanced in different terms, was offered by F. O. Matthiessen, who emphasized the nonhedonistic aspects of Stevens' poetry and expressed a considerably more sophisticated understanding of the "social" functions of that poetry than the judgment earlier set forth by Burnshaw:

The distinguishing trait of Stevens' late work is his deepening preoccupation with the problems of social order. He has not expressed a social philosophy so much as a many-sided awareness of disruption and breakdown. But that awareness, instead of crippling his energy, seems to have called out new resources, and his imagination has projected, under many guises, what integrity and coherence can mean. In response to the challenge of his wider themes, he has written much more than he did during the nineteen-twenties [Matthiessen may have been unaware that after *Harmonium* appeared Stevens published only two poems in the twenties], and his work, if losing some of its earlier dazzle, has taken on a dignity, an undertone of response to our most urgent human issues. This is what makes it more impressive in scope than that of any other poet writing in America.[41]

From the appearance of the "Wallace Stevens Number" until today, only three American critics of any prominence have taken serious issue with Matthiessen's view of Stevens' development. The first of these was Yvor Winters, who in 1943 published the essay "Wallace Stevens, or the Hedonist's Progress." Winters' moralistic theory of literature is by this time generally familiar: its central principle is that "the work of art, in so far as it is valuable, approximates a real apprehension and communication of objective truth,"[42] an apprehension common to "certain poetry of the sixteenth and seventeenth centuries" but increasingly rare since the eighteenth century.[43] There is a striking naïveté in the argument Winters sets forth in the "Foreword" to *Primitivism and Decadence,* for his bitterness against the modern poetry which fails to satisfy the cravings of his absolutism does not, as one might expect, lead him to consider what social and philosophical revolutions have occurred since the Renaissance which might account for the progressive relativism which he objects to in poetry.[44] Instead, he formulates three theories of literature which have come to replace the moralistic theory favored by him: the didactic, the hedonistic, and the romantic; and it is in the second of these categories that, as we might expect, he places Stevens.

According to the hedonistic ethics and hedonistic aesthetics (the two terms are more or less interchangeable for Winters), pleasure, which is the aim of life, consists in intensity of experience, in "the cultivation of the feelings for their own sake." For the hedonist aesthete, "literature . . . can provide a finer technique of such cultivation than can any other mode of activity." But unless hedontistic doctrines "have illicit relations with some non-hedonistic ethical theory we have no way of distinguishing among the many and diverse excitements that are commonly described as pleasurable." The plight of the hedonist, therefore, is an insatiable search for intensity of experience which, in turn, leads "to an endless pursuit of increasing degrees of violence of emotion or of increasingly elusive and more nearly meaningless nuances, and ultimately to disillusionment with art and with life."[45] Thus, whereas Matthiessen saw as "the distinguishing trait of Stevens' late work . . . his deepening preoccupation with the problems of social order," Winters finds there clearer and clearer symptoms of the final stages of hedonism, which for the poet is a fatal disease.

The apex of Stevens' art, in Winters' view, is "Sunday Morning." What is intriguing about this judgment—orthodox enough in itself—is first, that "Sunday Morning," published in 1915, is Stevens' second poem of fundamental importance—"Peter Quince at the Clavier" appeared a few months earlier—and second, that it defines, as Winters himself insists, the very hedonistic doctrines which were alleged to be the ruin of Stevens' art. Thus, it is "probably the greatest American poem of the twentieth century and . . . certainly one of the greatest contemplative poems in English";[46] but at the same time its subject is one which, "once formulated, and accepted as a guide to life and to expression, destroyed [Stevens'] style in less than two decades."[47] Inasmuch as Winters displays only limited sympathy with any other piece in *Harmonium,* we are puzzled both by his conclusion that Stevens "began as a great poet" and by the apparently over-generous two decades which he allows for the deterioration in style. In any event, it is Winters' opinion that by the mid-thirties Stevens was afflicted with the romantic ennui "which eventually overtakes the man who seeks for excitement instead of understanding,"[48] and from Stevens' own awareness of the futility of this perpetual search comes the progressive depression and irony of a man who "is unable to think himself out of the situation into which he has wandered."[49]

The degree of truth in Winter's argument has already received generous acknowledgment from Louis Martz, who wrote that "Winters has made a brilliant diagnosis of the malady; but he has underestimated the patient's will to live."[50] To this we might add, however, not only that Winters failed to perceive the antibodies already at work in *Harmonium,* but also that his impatience with Stevens' explicit atheism accounts to a degree for the unwarranted pessimism of his prognosis.

Winters' analysis of Stevens' alleged poetic breakdown was still finding supporters as late as 1949, when J. V. Cunningham discussed Stevens as an avant garde poet who "must exasperate his reader or succumb to him."[51] Probing less deeply than did Winters, Cunningham saw the result of this endless quest for the new, even when it helped to produce such poems as "Le Monocle de Mon Oncle," which he himself admired, to be a "poetry of a rare though too precious kind."[52] Through the brilliant analysis of "The Comedian as the Letter C" which is the basis for most of his judgments, Cunningham discovers the motivation for this preciosity in Stevens' disdain for the literary tradition and the society that nurtured him, and, finally, in a disdain for his readers, himself, and even poetry itself insofar as they belonged to that tradition and that society.[53]

The weakness of Cunningham's analysis, as of Winters', is that he neither sympathizes with nor understands the poetry which follows *Harmonium*, and that as a result of this failure he attempts to limit Stevens perpetually to the attitudes expressed in "The Comedian." Cunningham and Winters argue for a traditional poetry based on a set of absolute literary and ethical values; yet both critics seem unaware that while every important poet of our time has shared this preference, he has also insisted that the periods in which it could be satisfied are past. Rather than content himself to wish that Humpty Dumpty might be put together again, Stevens argued, like Yeats before him, that if the poet is to work once more within a systematic scheme, he must reconstruct one, and not pretend, as Cunningham would have him do, that the traditional religion and traditional order may still suffice.

The most recent and most brilliant diagnosis of Stevens' alleged poetic breakdown is that offered by Randall Jarrell. Although his greatest enthusiasm is reserved for the poems of the *Harmonium* period, Jarrell is far more sympathetic with Stevens' late work than were other members of his camp. Indeed, Jarrell's brief against Stevens is not in terms of philosophical failure but of philosophical aspiration. "The habit of philosophizing in poetry—or of seeming to philosophize, of using a philosophical tone, images, constructions, of having philosophical daydreams—has been unfortunate for Stevens," Jarrell believes.[54] The danger, he continues, is that poetry, whose essence is concreteness, will inevitably suffer from over-abstraction if it is made to carry philosophical burdens. (Whether Jarrell would have condemned *The Prelude* by these same standards, and how he would have reconciled this argument with his own admiration for Eliot's *Quartets,* are both questions which remain unspoken.) Increasingly in the later work, Jarrell believes, Stevens is without subjects sufficiently concrete to individualize his poems:

> Stevens has the weakness—a terrible one for a poet, a steadily increasing one for Stevens—of thinking of particulars as primarily illustrations of general truths, or else as aesthetic, abstracted objects, simply there to be contemplated; he often treats things or lives so that they seem no more than generalizations of an unprecedentedly low order. But surely a poet *has* to treat the concrete as primary, as something more than an instance, a hue to be sensed, a member of a laudable category—for him it is always the generalization whose life is derived, whose authority is delegated.[55]

In reply to the charge that "the habit of philosophizing in poetry . . . has been unfortunate for Stevens," we may well begin by quoting a philosopher who is also a literary critic. "It has, I feel sure, been nothing of the sort," writes Newton Stallnecht. "On the contrary, it has often supplied the orientation and the subject mat-

ter of his happiest verse."[56] May we not go still further
and insist that to object to Stevens' philosophizing is
equivalent to objecting to Wordsworth's nature worship,
Keats's sensualism, or, to change ground slightly, Pope's
couplets. "Wallace Stevens," as Northrop Frye has put
it, "was a poet for whom the theory and the practice of
poetry were inseparable. His poetic vision is informed
by a metaphysic; his metaphysic is informed by a theory
of knowledge; his theory of knowledge is informed by a
poetic vision."[57] In short, the habit of philosophizing
provides the very substance of Stevens' poetry, and although that habit becomes more explicit in the later
poetry, such early masterpieces as "Sunday Morning,"
"Le Monocle de Mon Oncle," "Thirteen Ways of Looking at a Blackbird," or, for that matter, that frigid classic,
"The Snowman," are all philosophical poems; and they
all, although to different degrees, treat the concrete not
as primary but as something which must be kept in
balance with the generalization it evokes. Here, then, we
may employ Newton Stallknecht's important distinction:
Stevens' poems about poetry, he writes, "are genuine
poetry of philosophical intention rather than ready-made
philosophical argument thrown into elegant verse."[58]
To put this in another way, they are poems whose subject is the very process of thought, the very movements
of the imagination—schizophrenic poems, like the
thoughts of dancers who observe themselves dancing.
To say that they are poems *about* poetry, although a
true statement, would be to violate the delicate fact,
for the preposition is inadequate to the relationship.
Like Yeats's "Sailing to Byzantium," Stevens' poems
about poetry simultaneously construct, contemplate, and
are the golden bird. More exactly still—as Stevens allowed one of these poems to define itself—

These are the edgings and inchings of final form,
The swarming activities of the formulae
Of statement, directly and indirectly getting at,

Like an evening evoking the spectrum of violet,
A philosopher practicing scales on his piano,
A woman writing a note and tearing it up.

It is not in the premise that reality
Is a solid. It may be a shade that traverses
A dust, a force that traverses a shade.[59]

The philosopher at his scales will never achieve the proficiency necessary to perform the ultimate concerto; the woman will never compose the ultimate note; for that concerto and that note are "the supreme fiction," the unachievable poem the theme of which is a teeming reality whose indefinability—not whose definition—accounts for the characteristic tentativeness of Stevens' most ambitious philosophical flights. It might be well here to insist on Stevens' own confusion on this score, a confusion reflected not only in such contradictions as I have already called attention to in the "Adagia," but also in the very title of his most concentrated assault on the concept, "Notes Toward a Supreme Fiction." We cannot but admire the integrity of Stevens' confusion, his intransigent refusal to sweep loose ends under the rug, his insistence to the very end of his career that he was that woman "writing a note and tearing it up." Stevens' conception of reality—and, I might add, of just what the poet must treat as primary—is labile as well as tentative; but the view that dominated his thought during the final decade of his life was less Platonic, more Berkleyan, than that which he had held earlier. "For all the assurances of the eye," he wrote in 1951, the material world has become immaterial. It has become an image in the mind. The solid earth disappears and the whole atmosphere is subtilized not by the arrival of some venerable beam of light from an almost hypothetical star but by a breach of reality. What we see is not an external world but an image of it and hence an internal world.[60]

If, as I believe, our willingness to embrace Stevens' concept of reality is no more essential to our appreciation of his poetry than it is in the case of Dante, or Yeats, or Eliot, we may find it necessary to assert less dogmatically that "a poet *has* to treat the concrete as primary." We may indeed be ready to concede that Stevens' later poetry, as Frank Doggett has put it, "finds its intensity in a passion for the straight look at that which is forever varying, uncertain, the nature of experience and its basis in reality."[61]

From this point of view, what Jarrell sees as "a terrible weakness" may better be understood as a means of expanding the dimensions of poetry. No longer content to allow metaphor to fulfill its own function, Stevens was increasingly intent in his later work to employ a technique he had experimented with as early as "Le Monocle de Mon Oncle." His task, as he came to understand it, was to communicate not only the defined poetic experience but also the process through which it reached definition. Thus, in the lines from "An Ordinary Evening in New Haven" which I quoted above, the first and third stanzas provide both abstract context and interpretation of the second. Before we too hastily object that it is the task of effective metaphor to speak for itself, we should recall that part of what Stevens is communicating is precisely the inadequacy of any metaphor to reflect accurately the reality which it evokes. The very tentativeness of the metaphor is thus a means of insisting that metaphoric definition is a Sisyphean task, that

> *It is not in the premise that reality*
> *Is a solid. It may be a shade that traverses*
> *A dust, a force that traverses a shade.*

It is because he conceived reality so that we must not expect from Stevens' poetry the pleasure which Yeats derived from the poem which closed like the click of a box's lid. Stevens' poetry only rarely takes the form of the well-wrought urn; but one of the peculiar pleasures which it does offer is the pleasure of our participation in the creative process, in seeing "a thought revolved,"— as one of Stevens' titles puts it—in watching over the woman's shoulder as she writes her note before tearing it up. Jarrell's complaint, in short, would seem to be a complaint against what Stevens conceived the modern poem to be:

> *The poem of the mind in the act of finding*
> *What will suffice.*

If Winters, Cunningham, and Jarrell, in their eagerness to advance poetic principles of their own, were in varying degrees insensitive to the aesthetic formulations Stevens himself had been working out since 1923, others were willing to judge what Stevens had done, rather than what, from their viewpoints, he should have been doing. The tenor of the criticism published since 1940 has been to put increasing emphasis on Stevens' philosophic and aesthetic positions, increasingly little on his hedonism.[62] Among the most important contributions to this body of criticism was a series of essays by Hi Simons which appeared from 1940 to 1946. Beginning with an exhaustive analysis of "The Come-

dian as the Letter C," Simons modified and expanded
his approach in articles on the three volumes of poetry
which Stevens published from 1942 to 1945. Against
those like Mary Colum, who complained of *Parts of a
World,* as Jarrell was later to complain of *Auroras of
Autumn,* that Stevens' absorption in philosophic speculation robs his poetry of sensual delight, Simons argued
that Stevens was a philosophic poet in the same sense as
was Donne, for whom, in Eliot's familiar characteriza-
tion, "a thought . . . was an experience; it modified his
sensibility." Stevens' poetry, Simons continued, similarly offers "a direct sensuous apprehension of thought,
or a recreation of thought into feeling."[63]

Although he thus assigned Stevens to that neo-
metaphysical school of modern poetry of which Eliot
himself is the leading representative, Simons was also
one of the first to discover in Stevens' work a kind of
poetic humanism of which Eliot has never been accused.
Stevens' humanism, Simons explained, is personified in
a poetic hero who contains "those capacities for nobler
living and thinking in which the average man transcends
himself."[64] Simons expanded this idea in a later essay,
where he wrote: "The poet is not to take precedence of
ordinary men, but all of us are to live ever more and
more by the imagination: as in every humanism, the
ideal is not humanity as it is, but a regenerated humanity."[65]

Simons' pioneer studies prepared the ground for
several other analyses of the coherence of Stevens'
oeuvre. Louis Martz has expressed disappointment that
because Stevens' "sceptical music offers no all-embracing
solution" he must "be placed a rung below Eliot and
Yeats." Nevertheless, Martz has shown that, in spite of
a development in Stevens' poetry toward increased abstraction and restraint, the central concern of that poetry

has always been the "continual renewing, by imaginative metamorphosis," of the poet's "relation to the world of physical objects."[66]

Marius Bewley and Roy Harvey Pearce are among other prominent critics who have attempted to trace the patterns of Stevens' poetic development. Unfortunately, the effectiveness of Bewley's essay is vitiated by several weaknesses. In contrasting *Harmonium* with such "mature" works as *Transport to Summer,* he ignores the fact that Stevens was forty-four when his first book was published, and that none of the poems in *Harmonium* seems to have been written much before his thirty-fifth year. Still more seriously damaging to Bewley's analysis is that, although he adroitly couples poems of the early period with parallel pieces from the later, he fails to provide any statement of the principles of coherence which unify Stevens' work. In his discussion of individual poems, Bewley is at times liable to patent misinterpretations, as when he suggests that the theme of "The Man Whose Pharynx is Bad" is "spiritual dejection," although both the title and the body of the lyric make it clear that it is a poem about not being able to write poetry.[67] These oversights, combined with Bewley's choice of admittedly inferior poems from *Harmonium,* not only lead him to provide a highly misleading impression of Stevens' poetic growth, but also to formulate a spurious demonstration of the thesis which he borrows from Marianne Moore: that "the interacting veins of life between [Stevens'] early and late poems are an ever-continuing marvel."[68]

Pearce's more ambitious and more successful essay traces the continuity and development of Stevens' theory of the imagination, a subject more recently handled in essays by Northrop Frye and Newton Stallknecht.[69] Pearce, who finds the fullest and most successful statements of this theory in "Notes Toward a Supreme Fiction" and "Esthétique du Mal," is concerned, like Simons, with the humanistic implications of Stevens' type of the imaginative man, "the major man," who raises to " 'the final elegance' even that man whom our religionists and rulers see as a poor bedraggled creature."[70]

Although this new insistence on Stevens' poetic humanism has at its roots Miss Moore's statement of three decades earlier—"The author's violence is for aggrandizement, not for stupor"—the critical trend has been anything but cyclical. Rather, in the critical history I have traced, we may discern three distinct and chronologically seriate approaches to Stevens' work. The first, advanced by Munson, Powys, Winters, and Cunningham, sees in Stevens a philosophically irresponsible hedonism and a socially irresponsible escapism which, to the more recent critics, seemed the cause of his eventual poetic decadence. The second, best set forth by Jarrell, sees a breakdown in Stevens' later work which results from his increasing absorption in philosophic speculation and in his sacrifice of the concrete to the general. The third, first sketched by Matthiessen and later developed by Simons, Pearce, and Martz, sees in the poetry of the thirties and into subsequent work "deepening preoccupation with the problems of social order" which was eventually to develop into a poetic humanism unique in the literature of our time.

Had it been my intention in this chapter to offer an exhaustive survey of the scholarship and criticism which has been devoted to Stevens during the past four decades, no small part of my discussion would have concerned such useful essays as those of Morton Zabel, Sister Bernetta Quinn, Frank Doggett, Michel Benamou, Joseph N. Riddel, Northrop Frye, John Crowe Ransom, and Samuel French Morse. It would also have been my responsibility to consider in detail William Van O'Connor's *The Shaping Spirit* and Robert Pack's *Wallace Stevens: An Approach to his Poetry and Thought,* the two earliest book-length studies devoted to Stevens. My concern, however, has been less to traverse each step of a critical path than to indicate its crucial turnings and thus to establish the direction in which it has been moving. Critics like Zabel and Morse have therefore received passing mention at best because their contributions are generally of a specialized kind which will demand attention in subsequent chapters.

My neglect of O'Connor and Pack is perhaps more regrettable; but neither of their books, I believe, offers critical insights which are not more cogently recorded elsewhere. Of the two books, O'Connor's is incomparably superior; but it suffers from inevitable limitations, both as a first book on its subject and as a study of a living writer whose work was far from completed. O'Connor's central concern is to provide introductory explanations of Stevens' meaning and method, explanations often guilty of a rambling superficiality which renders them useless to the careful reader. What today remains valuable in O'Connor's study is his first chapter and his last; the one, which discusses "Stevens as Legend," amasses the greater part of that small body of biographical information which Stevens had allowed to become available, and the other provides a rigorous examination of aspects of Stevens' poetic technique and the aesthetic which underlies it.

Whatever hope one may have entertained that Mr. Pack's study, published eight years after O'Connor's, might replace or at least supplement the pioneer work, is quickly disappointed, for Mr. Pack seems to have aimed at little more than a *jeu d'esprit,* a kind of romp through Stevensland. From the opening chapter, in which Pack insists that Stevens' mode is "comic" (this insistence unsupported by any awareness that Stevens' irony, humor, and self-satire appear most commonly in poems devoted to the theme of poetic sterility), to the last—in which he echoes jejune commonplaces regarding Stevens' fondness for archaisms, the irony and humor to be found in Stevens' titles, and the fact that "the reader seldom has the sense that a poem is addressed to a particular person or written about a special character"[71] —Pack reveals an irresponsibility toward his subject only more disappointing than his apparent ignorance of studies by Simons, Martz, Pearce, Morse, and others who might have helped him to substantiate or correct his own impressionistic commentary.[72]

The parent regrets his children's failure to know him. He has given them much, and they have taken it, and have forgotten its source; what he has best given, they have taken without knowing it was given, and possessed without knowing they had. These, it appears, were among Stevens' regrets in 1936, when, with that quality of intimate impersonality characteristic of his finest poems, he wrote "A Postcard from the Volcano":

> *Children picking up our bones*
> *Will never know that these were once*
> *As quick as foxes on the hill;*
>
> *And that in autumn, when the grapes*
> *Made sharp air sharper by their smell*
> *These had a being, breathing frost;*
>
> *And least will guess that with our bones*
> *We left much more, left what still is*
> *The look of things, left what we felt*

At what we saw. The spring clouds blow
Above the shuttered mansion-house,
Beyond our gate and the windy sky

Cries out a literate despair.
We knew for long the mansion's look
And what we said of it became

A part of what it is . . . Children,
Still weaving budded aureoles,
Will speak our speech and never know,

Will say of the mansion that it seems
As if he that lived there left behind
A spirit storming in blank walls,

A dirty house in a gutted world,
A tatter of shadows peaked to white,
Smeared with the gold of the opulent sun.[73]

The too blunt transition of the fourteenth line, the unfinished form of the three-line motif it introduces, even the all too easy grace of the poem's last line—these are the barely perceptible solecisms which passion controlled only at the expense of effort may momentarily execute on the most urbane speech.

From the voice of the father, however, we turn to the character of the children—the poets, critics, and others of the happy few whom large and patriarchal poets breed. It is the nature of such children to follow the example of the young Mark Twain, who, appalled at sixteen by his father's ignorance, was amazed at twenty-five to discover how much the old man had learned in the intervening nine years. In their earliest relations with the father, the children were indulgent but somewhat condescending toward the strange and vaguely admirable elder whose only real limitation was his failure to understand the world (even then, they knew, "a gutted world") as it is. He dwelt in a mansion furnished too lavishly for their tastes; their preference was for flats. He spoke an exotic tongue, which they admired but did not wholly understand; and then he stopped speaking it.

It was only in the following and harsher decade that he resumed speech, and now the family (an increasingly large one) was of several minds. Their only common ground was that the elder had suffered an assault by the Panzers of sordid reality. Their dispute was over his success in meeting it. One group maintained that his pleasure palace had proved no fit fortress, that the walls had crumbled, the fragility of the treasures been exposed by their ruin, in the midst of which maundered the shattered old man himself. The other group, more pious, insisted on a different account. The old man, they reported, stood amidst the wreckage of the palace he had built, gazed once around him, then buckled on the armor of Social Responsibility and attacked, crying: "It is a violence from within that protects us from a violence without." Although the Panzers continue to advance, and the old man is dead, the loyalists assign the victory to the vanquished. He spent his final days, they tell us, building anew; quoting another of their generals, they insist:

> *All things fall and are built again,*
> *And those that build them again are gay.*[74]

Stevens' poetic voyage, I suggested earlier, was a slow inclination from one pole to another, from a South which encouraged imaginative and philosophical self-indulgence to an austere North which made imperious demands. Having observed in outline how Stevens' critics have charted that voyage, we may now try our own hand.

II

A Most Inappropriate Man

I

To THOSE WHO YEARN for a peace between the artist
and society—confident that a truce would be to the ad-
vantage of both sides—the careers of Wallace Stevens
and William Carlos Williams have given great comfort.
Resisting the alternate allurements of the academies on
the one hand and of Ezra Pound's crankeries on the
other, Stevens and Williams steered a middle course by
pursuing respectable, categorically nonliterary careers in
business and medicine respectively, and devoted their
leisure hours to producing poetry of high merit. The
conclusion frequently drawn from their two examples
is that the contemporary artist may best resist the corrod-
ing elements of the quotidian world by immersing himself in them. Stevens himself, when he had grown
sufficiently large in stature to encourage reporters to
question him regarding his double life of insurance
executive and poet, remarked:

> It gives a man character as a poet to have daily con-
> tact with a job. If I lived an academic life in a col-
> lege, I don't believe I'd have half the reason for
> writing. This has been a life of my choice. I doubt

32

whether I've lost a thing by leading an exceedingly regular and disciplined life. I've never found it impossible to do about as much thinking and writing and reading as I want to do.[1]

To question a statement thrown out with such brisk executive authority may seem heretical; yet certain doubts continue to plague us. How does it occur, we wonder, that a poet whose work suggests exclusive preoccupation with the life of the imagination should have chosen to devote his working hours to a job so bleakly remote from the world of the imagination? And what effect, if any, had this seemingly heterodox choice of careers on Stevens' poetry itself? To dismiss these questions out of hand, as does William Van O'Connor when he tersely remarks: "There is nothing especially strange about a poet like Stevens dividing his life between insurance and poetry,"[2] is not only to cut ourselves off from whatever understanding of the character of the artist that might be gained by attempting to answer them, but also to deprive ourselves of a tool that may prove invaluable in unraveling some of the paradoxes which continue to surround Stevens' work. To arrive at this understanding and to gain possession of this tool is my object in tracing the pertinent outlines of Stevens' dual career and in reviewing some aspects of the strangeness that certain of his friends and admirers have discovered there. Once this is done, we shall be able to examine some of the symptoms of strain between poet and businessman that manifest themselves in the work of the *Harmonium* period, and perhaps to suggest why it was necessary that Stevens, in the closing years of his life, should wonder

> . . . *have I lived a skeleton's life,*
> *As a disbeliever in reality,*
> *A countryman of all the bones in the world?*[3]

A preliminary step faces us if we are to understand the apparent vagaries of Stevens' career and, thereby, the unexpected ambivalence that marks his attitude toward his art. The step takes us backward; for if, as I believe, Stevens' vocational dualism was reflected no less sharply in his work than was his philosophic dualism, he seems to have intended the violent yoking of mammonite and poet from the beginning. Indeed, in electing "to regard poetry as a form of retreat"—as in other critical elections—Stevens was walking in the footsteps of his father, Garrett Barcalow Stevens, a prominent Reading attorney.

In one of his adages, Wallace Stevens questioned: "Which is correct; whether, if I respect my ancestors I am bound to respect myself, or, if I respect myself, I am bound to respect my ancestors?"[4] We do not learn what answer he decided on, and it is probable that on this question, as on so many others, he was content to remain in doubt. Whatever the causal sequence, however, there can be no doubt that Stevens did feel a profound natural piety, as one of his rare autobiographical statements bears witness:

> My father was quite a good egg; agreeable, active. He was of Holland Dutch descent, and his father and his grandfather had been farmers. We had a good deal of poetry in the library. You might say we were more bookish than the average. We were all great readers and the old man used to delight in retiring to the room called the library on a Sunday afternoon to read a five-or-six-hundred-page novel. The library was no real institution, you understand; just a room with some books where you could go and be quiet. My mother just kept house

and ran the family. When I was younger, I always used to think that I got my practical side from my father and my imagination from my mother. I decided to be a lawyer the same way I decided to be a Democrat. My father was a lawyer, a Presbyterian and a Democrat.[5]

Whatever his mother may have contributed to Stevens' imaginative temperament, it is his heritage from his father that lends itself more clearly to our purpose. It was Garrett Stevens who enjoyed his literary Sunday afternoons, as his son was later to enjoy his Sunday mornings; and it was Garrett Stevens who, while a successful lawyer, was also "a writer of slight talent, who composed many poems, stories, and sketches, mostly for his own amusement." During the last years of his life, the elder Stevens' poems appeared anonymously in the Reading newspapers, and after his death in 1911 most of his writings were reprinted in *The Reading Times.*[6]

According to Michael Lafferty—and it would have delighted Stevens to learn that Lafferty's essay in the *Historical Review of Berks County* remains our sole source of information on these parallels between father and son—Garrett Stevens' poetry "is highly conventional, in the 19th-century tradition of Wordsworth, Longfellow, and Tennyson; it bears little resemblence to the avant garde poetry of his indirect and subtle son."[7] It is thus unlikely that even Stevens' piety could have won his admiration for his father's verse; for when, while he was a student at Harvard, he learned from Elsie Viola Kachel, whom he met in 1904 and married in 1909, that her favorite poet was Longfellow, he made the uncourtly remark: "My God, she said, 'Longfellow! Longfellow, a writer of nursery jingles!' "[8] On the other hand,

Stevens' own college poetry suggests that the difference between his early poetic taste and his father's may have been less sharp than the exclamation by the sophisticated Harvard undergraduate was probably intended to suggest. In any case, his paternal heritage included not only religion, political party, and profession, but also the avocation of poetry; as he later recalled with characteristic humility, he "wrote some poetry of a very elementary sort in his younger days, but nothing that had any significance."[9]

Although Stevens seems never seriously to have considered a career as an author, an observer of his formative years might well have thought him to be moving toward one. As a high school student he displayed a practical literary interest by working as a reporter for the *Reading Times* during vacations; and his high school acquaintances remember him "as a rather brilliant and creative, though shy young man,"[10] a judgment which precisely foreshadows those of the writers who were later to become acquainted with Stevens in New York City. These same early acquaintances further recall that during this period Stevens was unusually fond of reading poetry; and in an interview with Charles Henri Ford, Stevens himself listed among his early influences a high school friend who shared this affection: "they walked together, stopped, drank a bottle of claret together [a Keatsian taste no doubt symbolic], ate cheese, walnuts, and walking back home, this friend recited poetry—going through the woods—very loud. Very clear."[11]

Although Stevens had decided by 1897, when he entered Harvard, on a career in law, he was by this time already laying the foundation for the double life of his maturity. During his three years as a Harvard undergraduate, he published in the *Harvard Advocate*, under his own name and some half-dozen pseudonyms, a dozen poems, seven short stories, and, as president of the *Advocate* during the spring semester of 1900, fifteen editorials.

III

To look back at the early work of a major artist smacks somewhat of cheating at solitaire. The talent fulfilled speaks highly of that which first aspires, and we are easily flattered by historical perspective into mistaking modest gifts for early intimations of genius. Talent is after all the most delicate ingredient of genius, and it is a brash critic who will make long-range predictions on the basis of immature work.

The judicious reader of Stevens' earliest work would not have committed himself further than to wonder whether anything would come of an interesting talent. On this score Stevens could have assured him: nothing at all would come of it. Stevens wanted to be a lawyer, and, far worse, as he himself recalled some forty years later, he "wanted material success, wife, home, comforts."[12] He was, in short, another American undergraduate looking for security; and it is doubtful that he would have been much more impressed than most American undergraduates had he learned how the young Joyce, his near contemporary, was starving himself in Paris preparing for art, while Stevens played at poetry in Boston, preparing for comfort.

To Charles Henri Ford, Stevens was later to confess that "Maybe he wrote a bit of verse in Harvard, didn't take it seriously."[13] We may surmise that two quite different forces led him to assume early the dilettante's role which he continued, with diminishing persuasiveness, to play late. First, his father was a good egg who wrote a bit of verse in Reading, didn't take it seriously. For him, as for his son, poetry was an amusement in which one could indulge when one was not occupied with the practical affairs which made first claim on one's attention. The young Stevens admired his father, and it is natural that he should have followed him in this, as in so much else.

But another of Stevens' reminiscences has perhaps still more bearing on this point. "When I was here at Harvard a long time ago," Stevens observed to an audience in 1937, "it was a commonplace to say that all the poetry had been written and all the painting painted."[14] Such sentiments are indeed commonplace in our poetic tradition, and their debilitated resignation inevitably presages new literary revolt and the temporary revitalization which follows such revolt. For every half dozen poets willing to write once more what has already been written, there are always one or two obsessed with "making it new." Stevens was himself to become one of those who sought relentlessly the poem that had not already been written; as he put it toward the end of his life, "Newness (not novelty) may be the highest individual value in poetry. Even in the meretricious sense of newness a new poetry has value."[15]

Unfortunately, however, the *Harvard Advocate* of Stevens' day printed little, either in poetry or prose, to dispel the belief that if anything new *was* to be written, it would have to be written elsewhere. For connoisseurs of the short story, there were the vaguely Laurencian effusions of Frothingham Wells: "Ellen looked at Bradley in silence. His simple strength came home to her, as she watched him breathing full and fanning his healthy red cheeks."[16] The opening lines of the story "One Shall be Taken, The Other Left" make a different but no less direct appeal to the undergraduate who has been too long in college pent: "Bill and I were brothers.

Way up in the Hudson Bay country—where the wild geese honk as they fly to their northern breeding ground —and where the spruce logs come down on the spring freshets, we spent our happy, careless, boyish days."[17] This same primitive strain found poetic expression in Erskine Wood's "An Indian Lullaby," the first stanza of which defines the theme and tone:

> *Go to sleep, Eloutewa.*
> *Our tepee's red with the fire light.*
> *The coyotes howl in the snow tonight;*
> *But we are warm Eloutewa.*[18]

At the other extreme, the opening lines of Frederic Carleton Gulick's "Self-Consciousness," although perhaps caviar for the general, address themselves boldly to the man who reads good books:

> *In Hell's remotest rim there dwells a man*
> *Self-banned. The light of Virgil's eye*
>   *ne'er shone*
> *Upon him, ranging o'er dun fields alone,*
> *And Dante never saw his features wan.*[19]

Among this group of young writers who were doing badly what had better not have been done at all, Stevens must have attracted favorable attention by writing slight but polished exercises in what had often been done before. For the most part, his early verse is that of a young man who, having found no voice of his own, was attempting to imitate the various warbles of romantic and *fin-de-siècle* poets whom he admired. Adolescent isolation and melancholy which seek comfort in nature or in love is the theme which runs most heavily through these early lyrics, and the fondness for astronomical emblems which was later to be one of the foundations of Stevens' complex symbolism is here already strongly

marked. But even in the best of these conventional
etudes there is little to suggest that Stevens had this
early drunk of the milk of paradise. The vaguely Keatsian sonnet which he published in April 1899 illustrates
the characteristic mode of this early work at its best:

> *There shines the morning star! Through the*
> > *forlorn*
> *And silent spaces of cold heaven's height*
> *Pours the bright radiance of his kingly light,*
> *Swinging in revery before the morn.*
> *The flush and fall of many tides have worn*
> *Upon the coasts beneath him, in their flight*
> *From sea to sea; yet ever on the night*
> *His clear and splendid visage is upborne.*
>
> *Like this he pondered on the world's first day,*
> *Sweet Eden's flowers heavy with the dew;*
> *And so he led bold Jason on his way*
> *Sparkling forever in the galley's foam;*
> *And still he shone most perfect in the blue,*
> *All bright and lovely on the hosts of Rome.*[20]

Yet, if the sonnet offers no certain promise of genius, it
is nonetheless clearly the work of a talented young poet
who took it seriously enough while he wrote it. That
the diction is cliché-ridden is worth remarking, but once
remarked, this blemish need hardly detain us; it is a fact
generally recognized that the Muse's garden at the
turn of the century badly wanted weeding; and it is inevitable that we who have seen it hoed and trimmed
must take a less tolerant view of the romantic under-
growth than we would have found it necessary to take
six decades and more ago. More worthy of our notice
is the fluent rhythmic movement that carries us unfalter-
ingly to the effectively expansive line closing the poem.
Equally interesting in the light of Stevens' subsequent

poetic development is his preoccupation here and in other of the *Advocate* pieces with symbols of Olympian isolation. The peculiar reverence displayed toward the timeless, impersonal, and indifferent morning star will later find echoes in the well-known "Nuances on a Theme by Williams,"[21] and, more generally, in the quasi-religious posture which Stevens was later to adopt toward a nature he was reluctant to anthropomorphize.

Such thematic presages as these, however, although of some interest in retrospect, establish only the most tenuous lines of communication between this early work and that which was to come. Indeed, of the dozen lyrics Stevens published in the *Advocate*, only one, the "Ballade of the Pink Parasol," might immediately be recognized as the apprentice work of the author of *Harmonium*.

> *I pray thee where is the old-time wig,*
> *And where is the lofty hat?*
> *Where is the maid on the road in her gig,*
> *And where is the fire-side cat?*
> *Never was sight more fair than that,*
> *Outshining, outreaching them all,*
> *There in the night where lovers sat—*
> *But where is the pink parasol?*
>
> *Where in the pack is the dark spadille*
> *With scent of lavender sweet,*
> *That never was held in the mad quadrille.*
> *And where are the slippered feet?*
> *Ah! we'd have given a pound to meet*
> *The card that wrought our fall,*
> *The card none other of all could beat—*
> *But where is the pink parasol?*
>
> *Where is the roll of the old calash,*
> *And the jog of the light sedan?*

Whence Chloe's diamond brooch would flash
And conquer poor peeping man.
Answer me, where is the painted fan
And the candles bright on the wall;
Where is the coat of yellow and tan—
But where is the pink parasol?

Prince, these baubles are far away,
In the ruin of palace and hall,
Made dark by the shadow of yesterday—
But where is the pink parasol?[22]

Neither the strained pose of the undergraduate dandy nor such gaucheries of phrase as "poor peeping man" are likely to attract our serious attention to the ballade; but if we are listening for the first strains of *Harmonium*, it is here that we shall find them. Behind Stevens' light, even sophomoric irony there appears a Miniver Cheeveyan nostalgia which was later to provide in one guise or another, the *raison d'être* of his mature work. For Stevens, the primary function of the imagination was to transmute into gold some of the world's dross; but, unlike Eliot, whose poetry begins with the sordid and chaotic business of living and moves toward a formal perfection by whose means the sordid and chaotic may be surmounted, Stevens is likely to begin with images that are already transformations of the reality that suggests them. Poetry, in short, becomes not so much a reflection of what is as a movement toward what should be. Where this theory differs from formal Platonism is that no absolute claim for the reality of the mind's imaginings is made. Where it competes with theology is in raising the human imagination, as the power which can shape the world as it should be, to the kind of deity which it became for Blake.

Because Stevens has rarely made directly explicit

his discontent with the modern world, because he has published nothing comparable to *The Waste Land,* or *Mauberley,* or *The Age of Anxiety,* it is easy to forget what Randall Jarrell has acutely reminded us: "His poetry is obsessed with lack, a lack at last almost taken for granted, that he himself automatically supplies."[23] For Stevens, poetry was one of several kinds of connoisseurism by which he could store up within easy reach what in one of his letters he referred to as his "autumnal bon-bons."[24] As Lloyd Frankenberg suggests, "Wallace Stevens is a dilettant [sic]. He takes delight seriously."[25]

The particular interest of the youthful ballade is that it permits us to see two relationships in Stevens' work which have frequently been overlooked: first, that which connects his "dilettantism" to his obsession with "lack," and second, that which leads from this obsession with lack to the notoriously gaudy diction of the *Harmonium* period. Whereas R. P. Blackmur would have us believe that the abundant archaisms and euphuisms of this poetry are merely the reflections of a laudable passion for the right word, it is in fact important to insist on what Mr. Blackmur denies: Stevens *does* frequently choose uncommon words as elegant substitutes for plain terms,[26] and he chooses them because of his acute dissatisfaction with the plainness which even in 1900 seemed to him characteristic of our time and place. Whereas Eliot and his followers sought to restore poetry by restricting themselves to a plain, "nonpoetic" diction, Stevens insisted that the passion for elegance was the very seed of poetry:

> If the desire for resemblance is the desire to enjoy reality, it may be no less true that the desire to enjoy reality, an acute enough desire today, is the desire for elegance. Euphuism had its origin in the

43

desire for elegance and it was euphuism that was a reason in the sun for metaphor.[27]

Viewing the ballade within the confines of this subsequently elaborated framework, we perceive that through the "wigs" and "gigs," the "spadilles" and "quadrilles," the "Chloes" and "calashes," diction itself becomes a device, however feeble, for restoring lost elegance, as if the sounds of the words could provide at least limited solace for the loss of the things.

We need only take one step further to perceive also that for Stevens the desire for elegance was an aspect of a still more basic desire for nobility. The dilemma which Stevens set forth in "The Noble Rider and the Sound of Words," his most direct essay at the restoration of the concept of nobility, would now appear to be one that concerned him from earliest maturity:

> There is no element more conspicuously absent from contemporary poetry than nobility. There is no element that poets have sought after, more curiously and more piously, certain of its obscure existence. Its voice is one of the inarticulate voices which it is their business to overhear and to record. The nobility of rhetoric is, of course, a lifeless nobility. Pareto's epigram that history is a cemetery of aristocracies easily becomes another: that poetry is a cemetery of nobilities. For the sensitive poet, conscious of negations, nothing is more difficult than the affirmations of nobility and yet there is nothing that he requires of himself more persistently, since in them and in their kind, alone, are to be found those sanctions that are the reasons for his being and for that occasional ecstasy, or ecstatic freedom of the mind, which is his special privilege.[28]

Behind the sincere high-mindedness lingers a festering doubt, itself the register of Stevens' own consciousness of negations: "The nobility of rhetoric is, of course, a lifeless nobility"; yet, if this is so, how is it that Stevens can claim, as he does at the close of his essay, that because the imagination seems "to have something to do with our self-preservation . . , the expression of it, the sound of its words, helps us to live our lives"?[29] As will become increasingly apparent in the course of this study, Stevens' obsessive questioning of the reality of the imagination's artifacts has as its motive the fear that poetry may offer no other but this lifeless nobility of rhetoric, in which case the desire for elegance points the way not to affirmations of nobility but to nostalgia for pink parasols. Thus the ballade not only introduces us to an aesthetic quandary with which Stevens was to struggle to the end of his life, but it also foreshadows the ambivalent self-mockery which we will in a moment study in *Harmonium.*

IV

When, in 1950, Stevens was confronted by the poetry of his first period in the pages of the *Harvard Advocate Anthology,* his reaction was brief and characteristically succinct and modest: "Some of one's early things give one the creeps," he remarked.[30] Yet he had won a certain literary success at Harvard, where, as editor of the *Advocate,* he wrote and published "a good deal of the material to keep it going."[31] Whether as a result of this local reputation or because his part-time work on Reading newspapers had awakened his interest in journalism, upon leaving Harvard he entered, for the first and last time, the world of professional writing: he became a reporter for the *New York Tribune.*[32] Of

Stevens' career as reporter only one anecdote has come down; in William Carlos Williams' words:

> There is also the story of the down and out Stevens sitting on a park bench at the Battery watching the outgoing tide and thinking to join it, as a corpse, on its way to the sea (he had been a failure as a reporter). As he sat there watching the debris floating past him he began to write—noting the various articles as they passed. He became excited as he wrote and ended by taking to the Tribune office an editorial or "story" that has become famous—in a small way, among newspaper offices. . . .[33]

Although it may have saved Stevens from the outgoing tide, the editorial did little to extend Stevens' newspaper career; for in the fall of 1901 he entered the New York Law School, from which he graduated in 1903. From that point on Stevens advanced unwaveringly toward the material comforts he had earlier chosen as his goal, and his legal career seems never to have suffered the viccisitudes that were to mark his poetic avocation. Although nothing Stevens may have written during this period has been preserved, or at least, can be identified, "his business associates recall that he was writing poetry at that time; however, they admit that they did not understand every word of it."[34] It would thus appear that Stevens' double life of insurance executive and poet had its roots in the very beginning of his professional career.

While Stevens remained thus withdrawn from a literary world which he had scarcely entered, that world was changed utterly, and the terrible beauty of a new poetry was being born. By 1914 Ezra Pound was in London kindling the sparks of a new literary renascence with such frenetic energy that parallel efforts to kindle new lights on American soil are even today underestimated by most literary historians. Yet in Greenwich Village the home fires were burning vigorously in 1914, and among the minor lights who had been drawn to the scene by the prospect of a conflagration were several of Stevens' college friends—among them, Walter Arensberg, Pitts Sanborn, and Witter Bynner. Stevens was living in New York City at this time, and through these old acquaintances he was drawn into the circle of Village writers and artists. Perhaps under the influence of their conversation and their achievements, perhaps because in gaining a wife—he was married in 1909 —and material security he now felt free to indulge in the luxury of poetry, he made at the age of thirty-five, an uncharacteristically dramatic entrance on the literary stage. As Harriet Monroe recalls the event:

> We had selected for [a special War Number of *Poetry*] thirteen poems of war from seventeen-hundred-and-thirty-seven submitted in the competition for our one-hundred-dollar prize, and had even paged up the proof, when a new and irresistible claimant arrived, and we had to squeeze out two more pages for a group of *Phases* by one Wallace Stevens, a name then unfamiliar.[35]

The irresistible claimant which so fired Miss Monroe's enthusiasm consisted of a series of skilfully wrought pieces, largely patterned after the imagistic method, and reflecting such attitudes toward war as those which the young Henry Fleming (of Crane's novel) held while he was still at a distance from it. Section IV of the published version is typical both of the delicate technique which inspired Miss Monroe to scrawl "Jewel" across the top of the manuscript[36] and of the naive callousness with which Stevens sought to transmute into poetic elegance, even nobility, the dross of a rapidly spreading World War:

Death's nobility again
Beautified the simplest men.
Fallen Winkle felt the pride
Of Agamemnon
When he died.

What could London's
Work and waste
Give him—
To that salt, sacrificial taste?

What could London's
Sorrow bring—
To that short, triumphant sting?[37]

It is a tribute to Miss Monroe's own taste that among the sections she declined to publish was the one which began with the singularly unmilitary reflection:

Peace means long, delicious valleys
In the mode of Claude Lorraine. . . .[38]

and it was apparently at her suggestion also that the poem was published under Stevens' name, although it had been submitted under the shockingly inappropriate pseudonym, "Peter Parasol."[39] If this attempt to beat spears into pink parasols was characteristic of the War Number of *Poetry*, D. H. Lawrence's reaction was a temperate one indeed when, upon receipt of the issue, he wrote to Miss Monroe:

> Today came the War Number of *Poetry*, for which I also thank you. It put me into such a rage —how dare Amy talk about bohemian glass and stalks of flame?—that in a real fury I had to write my war poem, because it breaks my heart, this war.
>
> I hate, and hate, and hate the glib irreverence of some of your contributors. . . .[40]

Although "Phases" must undoubtedly have contributed fuel to Lawrence's hot indignation, it proved also to constitute a significant victory for American poetry. For all his professed indifference to both public and critics, Stevens has provided abundant evidence that he was keenly sensitive to both. If we cannot now determine the importance Stevens may have attached to this acceptance by the most highly respected poetry journal of the period, we can at least surmise that it encouraged him, probably for the first time, to think of himself seriously as a writer. Between November 1914, when "Phases" appeared in *Poetry,* and September 1923, when *Harmonium* was released, Stevens published nearly a hundred poems and two verse dramas, surely a frantic rate of production for a man who had managed to remain silent for fourteen years.

v

In 1940, Charles Henri Ford contributed engagingly to the Wallace Stevens legend by inquiring in a subtitle, "Has the Mystery Man of Modern Poetry Really Another Self?" Apparently lending himself to the spirit evoked by the inquiry, Stevens, at the close of his interview with Ford, enjoined: "Make me look romantic in those photographs."[41] As far as one can judge, Ford did his best to comply; the photograph which accompanies his article represents a portly man in dark suit and tie, his figure half obscured by a sprinkling of giant peonies each as big as his head, but his Gioconda smile scarcely convincing enough to disguise the familiar prototype of the successful businessman's face which it cradles.

The juxtaposition of business executive and aesthete in Stevens has fascinated businessmen and aesthetes alike. As *Business Week* put it, bluntly but with quiet pride over another home town boy who made good, "Wallace Stevens is probably the only vice-president in the country who is also a first-rate poet."[42] Not so very different was the reaction of Harold Loeb, who, recalling a memorable evening that he, as an aspiring young aesthete, had spent in the company of Burton Rascoe, Scofield Thayer, William Carlos Williams, and Stevens, wrote: "I enjoyed them all, but Stevens held me spellbound. He looked like a football player, wrote poetry, was successful in business, and had a biting wit. I was happy to shed the delusion that business and poetry were incompatible."[43] Although far less wide-eyed, Alfred Kreymborg was no less fascinated by this strange figure of mammonite as artist: "To the yearning national question, where is our next major poet to come from," he wrote in 1929, when there seemed little reason to hope that Stevens would return to poetry, "I always feel like responding: Out of Wallace Stevens, if Stevens would let him come. But the exasperating fellow sticks to his laws and lawyers."[44]

What disturbed Kreymborg, of course, was not simply that Stevens had chosen to practice law, but that in some respects he displayed toward poetry the characteristic indifference of the man of affairs. Much has been made, by Kreymborg and others, of Stevens' reluctance to publish a first book, and we are led to believe that when he finally did so it was only at the insistence of his friends, especially of Carl Van Vechten. As one account has it, his motive for consenting was that he was "bored with being the sole poet who had refused to publish a book,"[45] but in a letter to William Carlos Williams, Stevens less cavalierly remarked, "Well a book of poems is a damned serious affair."[46]

As we shall see in a moment, it was in fact a profound respect for the seriousness of the undertaking

rather than a cavalier indifference that inspired Stevens'
reluctance to publish. To those of his contemporaries
who were unable to determine his motivation, however,
the aura of mystery which surrounded Stevens deepened
when his initial distaste for publishing books was re-
placed, after the release of *Harmonium,* by an uncom-
promising refusal to publish at all. In Kreymborg's
words, "Formerly it was impossible to get him to publish
a book; now it is impossible to get him to publish a poem.
Write him, wire him or see him, one always receives
the same answer: he has written nothing for years."[47]

It was, however, neither Stevens' apparent indifference to publication nor his desertion, during the twenties, of art for law which alone inspired the Wallace
Stevens legend. Even for those literary people who
knew him best in the late teens and early twenties,
Stevens seemed a distant, if not an exotic figure. Although he occasionally attended literary parties in
Greenwich Village, he generally remained at the social
periphery:

> Everybody knew him, knew him well—but he
> never said much. He was always the well dressed
> one, diffident about letting down his hair. Precise
> when we were sloppy. Drank little. . . . But we all
> knew, liked and admired him. He really was felt to
> be a part of the gang.[48]

This is Williams' recollection, and it corresponds closely to that of Kreymborg, who relates how, on one of the
rare occasions when Stevens was inspired to recite one
of his poems to a group of friends, he "waited for conversation to reach a fairly confused height before he
drew forth a paper that looked like a poem but sounded
like a tête-à-tête with himself.[49] Kreymborg provides a
still more striking illustration of Stevens' diffidence with

his account of a walk the two took together on "one of the occasions when [Stevens] came down from Hartford":

> So slight was Krimmie alongside Wallace that the latter was fond of guiding him across crowded thoroughfares and protecting him against the traffic. On one of these walks, the giant suddenly stuffed a package into his editorial pocket, with the hasty proviso: "I must ask you not to breathe a word of this. Print it if you like it, send it back if you don't." It was the manuscript—in the most minute handwriting—of the now famous poem, Peter Quince at the Clavier.[50]

If to some, like Kreymborg, it appeared that Stevens "wore his self-deprecation as a protective mantle,"[51] to others, like Paul Rosenfeld, Stevens seemed to be a Pierrot—Hamlet and clown—whose poetry gave the impression that "What he has to say appears too useless for him to say it out."[52] Gradually these various views fuse into a single image, the doubly paradoxical image of, on the one hand, the diffident business executive, and, on the other, the poet wary of communication, wary of publication. It is no wonder that Amy Lowell, viewing "the mystery man of modern poetry" from a greater distance than these others, drew him in doggerel as an enigmatic character indeed:

> *There's another young man who strums a clavier*
> *And prints a new poem every third or fourth year.*
> *Looking back, I don't know that anything since*
> *Has delighted me more than his 'Peter Quince.'*
> *He has published no books and adopts this as pose,*
> *But it's rather more likely, I think, to suppose*
> *The particular gift he's received from the Muses*
> *Is a tufted green field under whose grass there oozes*

A seeping of poetry, like wind through a cloister;
On occasion it rises, and then the field's moister
And he has a poem if he'll trouble to bale it,
Address it to 'Poetry' and afterwards mail it.
His name, though the odds overbalance the evens
Of those who don't know it as yet's Wallace Stevens,
But it might be John Doe for all he seems to care—
A little fine work scattered into the air
By the wind, it appears, and he's quite unaware
Of the fact, since his motto's a cool 'laisser-faire.'[53]

William Van O'Connor considers many of the anecdotes which surrounded Stevens during these years to be apocryphal, and they may well be. Certainly Stevens' own statements have relentlessly stripped his divided life of any mystery; and when Lewis Nichols raised the inevitable question in an interview that took place a year before Stevens' death, he replied:

> I prefer to think I'm just a man, not a poet part time, businessman the rest. This is a fortunate thing, considering how inconsiderate the ravens are. I don't divide my life, just go on living.[54]

To an observer less authoritative than Stevens himself, however, it would appear that he was indeed a poet part time, businessman the rest. From his twenty-second to his thirty-fifth year, while he was making his reputation as a lawyer, he published nothing. Then, between 1914 and 1923, Stevens published nearly 100 poems and wrote three plays in verse, two of which were performed, although neither with great popular success.[55] In July 1924, he published "Sea Surface Full of Clouds," which, if somewhat debilitated in spirit, showed no waning of either craft or sensibility. The following month there appeared only "Red Loves Kit," which Stevens excluded from all published collections during his lifetime.[56] The

lyric, which starts from the ephemeral sentiments recorded in chalk on a sidewalk,[57] and moves through
evoked archaic romanticism to an art "fecund in apt
curios," seems to point toward a new engagement of the
bleak realities of the North, of the "slime of men in
crowds" which, in the later "Farewell to Florida,"
Stevens felt that he must confront in order to achieve
poetic freedom.[58] But, "Red Loves Kit" proved to be
a renunciation, not a transition. Only in 1930 did
Stevens begin to publish again, and only in 1934 was
he once more producing in volume.

The renunciation of poetry by a writer who has
completed one phase of his development and seems
about to enter another is, although not without parallel,
sufficiently unusual to engage our attention. There had
already been a clear hint of it in "The Comedian as the
Letter C," which Samuel French Morse aptly describes
as "a kind of *summa poemarum* of all that precedes it."[59]
Crispin, the poetic hero of "The Comedian," begins
his allegorical voyage in search of a rounded aesthetic
but ends in defeat, resigned to the doctrine:

> *The words of things entangle and confuse.*
> *The plum survives its poems.*[60]

From which point, although the road to meditation remains open, the straiter path to creation would appear
to be closed. The birth of a daughter, Holly, in 1924, as
well as business responsibilities which required him to
travel widely and frequently, were among the quotidian
affairs which cut deeply into Stevens' time and interest
during this period. In addition to these considerations,
the popular reception of *Harmonium,* whose first edition sold fewer than one hundred copies, could hardly
suggest to Stevens that the public was clamoring for his
work. As he wrote to Harriet Monroe with mordant

wit: "My royalties for the first half of 1924 amounted to $6.70. I shall have to charter a boat and take my friends around the world."[61]

Had Stevens' relations with his own art been easy, however, it is doubtful that any of these considerations would have kept him from it. In point of fact they were not easy. The skepticism regarding the significance of poetry which we have already remarked in "The Comedian" was deep-rooted in Stevens and, as we shall see later, not only helped to inspire the ironies of the first volumes but was also responsible in part for the ambitious metaphysical claims of the later work.

The elements of this uneasy marriage between art and business are many and complex, and we would be serving banality but not truth by attributing to any one of them the trial separation that followed. Stevens' letters of this period do suggest, however, that the essential conflict which led to the temporary triumph of the quotidian was relatively simple. On the one hand, he had mastered the by no means simple instrument to which for ten years he had applied himself, and its music no longer satisfied him; only new tunes on a bigger keyboard could now suffice. On the other, having committed himself to securing what was as important to him as his art, and in a peculiar way related to it—the material comfort which wealth alone could bring—he found it impossible to devote to the new instrument the unbroken attention necessary to master it.

Hints of the conflict begin to appear in the fall of 1922, just after Stevens had finished rewriting "The Comedian." "When I get back from the South," he wrote to Harriet Monroe in September,

> I expect to do some short poems and then to start again on a rather longish one; so that sooner or later

I shall have something for Poetry, to which I send what I like most. But it takes time, and, besides, I have no desire to write a great deal. I know that people judge one by volume. However, having elected to regard poetry as a form of retreat, the judgment of people is neither here nor there. The desire to write a long poem is not obsequiousness to the judgment of people. On the contrary, I find that this prolonged attention to a single subject has the same result that prolonged attention to a senora [sic] has, according to the authorities. All manner of favors drop from it. Only it requires a skill in the varying of the serenade that occasionally makes me feel like a Guatemalan when one wants to feel like an Italian. I expect that after a while Crispin . . . will become rudimentary and abhorrent.[62]

Five weeks later, when Stevens was at work assembling the manuscript of *Harmonium*, the conflict came into sharper focus:

Gathering together the things for my book has been so disagreeable that I wonder at Poetry's friendliness. All my earlier things seem like horrid cocoons from which later abortive insides have sprung. [Stevens would, incidentally, elaborate on this image in the poem "Ghosts as Cocoons," which he published fourteen years later.] The book will amount to nothing, except that it may teach me something. I wish that I could put everything aside and amuse myself on a larger scale for a while. One never gets anywhere in writing or thinking unless one can do long stretches at a time. Often I have to let go, in the most insignificant poem, which scarcely serves to remind me of it, the most skyey of skyey sheets. And often when I have a real fury for indulgence I must stint myself. . . . The reading of these outmoded and debilitated poems does make me wish rather desperately to keep on dabbling and to be as obscure as possible until I have perfected an authentic and fluent speech for myself. By that time I should be like Casanova at Waldstein with nothing to do except to look out the windows.[63]

It would appear that by this time the projected long poem had dwindled to an amusement which one could not afford. And against Stevens' desire to perfect "an authentic and fluent speech," we must weigh the self-mockery of "dabbling"; against his ambition to depict on adequate canvas that ultimate skyey sheet—as an emblem of ultimate reality the subject eluded him to the end—we must balance his unwillingness to pay, as did Casanova, the cost.

Thus, if with part of his mind Stevens hoped that through temporary obscurity he might perfect his art, with another he wanted to be done, for the time being at least, with poetry altogether. That he made no conscious decision to act on the promptings of either part is evident from the handful of letters he wrote to Louis Untermeyer from 1925 to 1929. When, early in 1925, the anthologist asked him for a new poem, Stevens was still hoping, although without great enthusiasm, to produce one. "I am sorry not to have received your letter from Vienna," he wrote.

> If I am expected to say definitely that I will have something in your hands by March 1, I shall have to be counted out. If, however, I am merely expected to say that I shall try to have something in your hands by that time, well and good.
> There are a great many things cutting in now-

adays. There is a baby and a radio, and I am expecting to go to Florida in a week or so, etc.[64]

The baby and the radio, which Stevens also listed in a letter to Harriet Monroe as distractions—the former, who "babbles and plays with her hands and smiles like an angel,"[65] not, clearly, an unwelcome one—were apparently relentless in their obstructionism; for when six weeks later Stevens offered to send Untermeyer a poem, it was "Sea Surface Full of Clouds," first published a year earlier; Stevens at the same time made it clear that Untermeyer could expect nothing new: "I have been too much on the go to do any writing. I thought it might be possible to do something when I was South, but it was not."[66] In the fall of 1926, Stevens' mood was gayer, but his refusal no less definite:

> It doesn't in the least look as though I should have anything for your annual this year. At the present time all my attention is devoted to reducing, getting the week's washing done (not by me but by one of the ever-flitting laundresses of the town), etc.
>
> I see a vast amount of nature, my source of supply, but I am obliged to see it at the rate of about six miles an hour, and not even a honey bee could do much business at that gait.[67]

Only in the summer of 1929 was the indefatigable litterateur able to win a handout from the quick-stepping entrepreneur; in June of that year Stevens sent Untermeyer a copy of "Annual Gaiety," which appeared in all subsequent editions of Untermeyer's *Modern American Poetry* but which Stevens never included in a book.

Although "Annual Gaiety" offers no hint of that "authentic and fluent speech" which seven years earlier

Stevens had hoped to achieve, and although, as late as August 1932, he could assure Miss Monroe that "Whatever else I do, I do not write poetry nowadays,"[68] the poem proved to be the first presage of Stevens' poetic renascence, the causes of which are as complex as those which led him to set his poetry aside in 1924. For the moment, we may offer in tentative explanation, first, Stevens' solidly established business reputation, which allowed him more time and thought for the art which to him was essentially a leisure activity; second, the warm critical reception of the second edition of *Harmonium*, which appeared in 1931; and third, paradoxically, the violent social and economic upheavals of the thirties. In a peculiar sense, John Gould Fletcher's dark prophecy had been accurate after all: "But for the future," Fletcher had written in 1923, "he must face a clear choice of evils: he must either expand his range to take in more of human experience, or give up writing altogether. 'Harmonium' is a sublimation which does not permit of a sequel."[69] In *Harmonium,* Stevens brought an old world into at least a precarious equilibrium, and it was somehow only when that equilibrium and that world itself came to an end that Stevens could carve new poems out of new chaos.

VI

When in 1955 Stevens remarked to the *Time* magazine reporter who was interviewing him, "It gives a man character as a poet to have daily contact with a job," the reporter must certainly have nodded his head in judicious approval. "At least he isn't one of those artists who pretend that art *is* a job," he may have mused. If he did, he was at least half right. Stevens, as we have seen, indulged his appetite for writing poetry in the same way that another executive might indulge his appetite for fishing—he wrote when quotidian demands were not pressing, and, as it were, when the weather was good. Similarly, Stevens has expressed attitudes toward poetry which might heartily be endorsed by his own business associates or by Mr. Luce himself. "The poetic process is psychologically an escapist process," we have heard him remark.[70] "That is what we have said all along," we can fancy a chorus of mammonites replying. He had decided "to regard poetry as a form of retreat," he wrote to Harriet Monroe on September 23, 1922; and again we hear the chorus chanting in response: "As long as you don't pretend that it is anything else, enjoy it, although speaking for ourselves, we prefer to fish."

My point is not simply facetious. Just as it may be argued that for Stevens all life is a metaphor for poetry, so may it be argued that his own life is a particularly vivid metaphor for his own poetry. What, after all, are the two selves that comprised Stevens' double life? On the one hand, the mammonite: successful at business, practical-minded, serving a respected and responsible social function. Not all business, of course, for we are dealing no longer with the primitive mammonite who inspired Victorian jeremiads; the new breed is capable of finding relief from the pressures of "reality" in the collecting of *objets d'art* and paintings, even in the writing of poetry.

Setting aside for the moment the fact that he was a major poet—and to be sure that is a large fact to set aside—Stevens shared many characteristics with these new mammonites. Like them, he was frequently willing to allow his agents, both amateur and professional, to do his collecting for him. Through one such agent, a Paris art dealer, he acquired such second-rank French impressionists as he could afford. And from friends who traveled to more distant places than the Florida Keys, where he preferred to vacation, he received occasional surprise packages in which he took almost childish delight. Thus, in the letter written in 1922 to Miss Monroe he expressed his keen pleasure over a package of jasmine tea which Miss Monroe's sister had sent him from Peking; it provided him an opportunity to smell "one of the good smells out of China. It is a very good smell indeed and I am delighted. Nothing could please me more." The tea, with the jade screen and carved figures which came with it, offered him, he remarked, a "blissful adventure." It is in the same letter that Stevens spoke of his friend Pitts Sanborn, who was about to sail from Le Havre, "bringing for me my autumnal bon-bons from the Place de l'Opéra, not to speak of a number of books etc. which he has picked up for me."[71] In 1935, when Miss Monroe's sister was again in China, Stevens prepared for another blissful adventure by requesting that she purchase for him, "say, a pound of Mandarin Tea, a wooden carving, a piece of porcelain or one piece of turquoise, one small landscape painting, and so on and so on."[72] In his next letter, however, he wrote that he would rather leave the selection to the sister, "with the general remark that what I want the things for is not to place them on the mantlepiece, say, but to do me good."[73] In short, Jarrell was more astute than he could have known when he saw in one aspect of Stevens' poetic character a kind of J. P. Morgan of modern poetry, who "likes something, buys it (at the expense of a little spirit), and ships it home."[74]

For the mammonite connoisseur, indulgence in art requires neither social nor metaphysical justification. The amateur collector, the Sunday painter or the Sunday poet, is motivated by nothing more complex than pleasure, and if asked why he collects, or paints, or poetizes, he can readily explain that he simply enjoys doing so. He need not justify his taste to others nor, if he creates, need he communicate with any audience. For him culture is what Josef Pieper has defined as "the quintessence of all the natural goods of the world and of those gifts and qualities which, while belonging to man, lie beyond the immediate sphere of his needs and wants."[75] Where he differs from the professional, of course, is that for the latter art itself is at the center of the immediate sphere of needs and wants.

One side of Stevens' temperament led him to the position of the amateur, for whom art need supply nothing more grand than pleasure, and to that of the Philistine, who is likely to become impatient with an art that claims to provide more than amusement. Another side, however, could be satisfied with nothing less than a poetry which illuminated the very substance of reality, and a theory of the imagination, essentially melioristic, which might make the life of the imagination a possible life even for the "mickey mockers" who now scorn it.[76]

It is the conflict between these two temperaments that accounts for the wide range of misconceptions that Stevens' early work inspired. As Willard Thorp has remarked, it is not surprising that it took so long for Stevens' work to win readers when, confronted by the collage-like poetry common to the early period, they were led to wonder "How did these odd fragments fit together, or, if they did, would the whole thing add up to a joke sprung on the reader? At times Stevens seemed to be a very serious poet indeed but how could one be sure when the titles of his poems were often whimsical or nonsensical?"[77]

The solution to the basic problem raised by Thorp, we may now suggest, is that although no one since Matthew Arnold has made higher claims than Stevens for

the intrinsic value and the potentially melioristic function of poetry, no one has, at the same time, so taken
to heart the sort of indictment which Thomas Love
Peacock made of "the iron age of modern poetry": "A
poet in our times," Peacock wrote,

> is a semi-barbarian in a civilized community. He
> lives in the days that are past. His ideas, thoughts,
> feelings, associations, are all with barbarous man-
> ners, obsolete customs, and exploded superstitions.
> The march of his intellect is like that of a crab,
> backwards. The brighter the light diffused around
> him by the progress of reason, the thicker is the
> darkness of antiquated barbarism, in which he
> buries himself like a mole, to throw up the barren
> hillocks of his Cimmerian labours. . . . The highest
> inspirations of poetry are resolvable into three in-
> gredients: the rant of unregulated passion, the
> whining of exaggerated feeling, and the cant of
> facetious sentiment: and can therefore serve only
> to ripen a splendid lunatic like Alexander, a puling
> driveller like Werter, or a morbid dreamer like
> Wordsworth. It can never make a philosopher, nor
> a statesman, nor in any class of life an useful or
> rational man. It cannot share in any one of the
> comforts and utilities of life of which we have
> witnessed so many and so rapid advances.[78]

Stevens was at least an occasional subscriber to
Peacock's view, and the whimsy and nonsense to which
Thorp alludes are the result of his erratic tendency to
reduce the conflict between reality and the imagination
to one between "the real business of life," on the one
hand, and splendid lunacy, puling drivel, or morbid
dreams on the other. That poetry which one of his titles
describes as a "Holiday in Reality"[79] on occasion ap-

peared to him ominously close to the holiday from reality enjoyed by the soma-eating Brave New Worlders. Indeed, this parallel goes further, for in Stevens' darker moods, as in the occasional funks of Huxley's unhappy utopians, reality is reduced to the violent and the sordid, and the tragic function of the poet, who in this aspect is Peacock's morbid dreamer, is to resist or evade "the pressure of the reality of this last degree, with the knowledge that the degree of today may become a deadlier degree tomorrow."[80]

Here, then, is a crucial paradox which stems directly from the double life of mammonite and poet which Stevens chose to pursue: the fervid acolyte of the imagination offers us a figure of the poet as quixotic museum curator for a barbaric age. His plaintive motto:

> *Shall I grapple with my destroyers*
> *In the muscular poses of the museums?*
> *But my destroyers avoid the museums.*[81]

Stevens, of course, has simply reversed the value judgment implicit in Peacock's argument; for him, as for the majority of his peers, only the "semi-barbarians" inhabit the "civilized community." Objective reality, from the viewpoint of that community, is reduced to things as they unsatisfyingly are, and the real world more closely resembles the offices of the Hartford Accident and Indemnity Company than it does the fecund dream-world of the American tropics. Reality, in short, becomes what the businessman thinks it is, and the poet is left to make his lonely claims in solipsistic song:

> *. . . things are as I think they are*
> *And say they are on the blue guitar.*[82]

I do not wish to suggest that either Stevens' case or our own rests here with the belief that the final resistance to the pressure of reality is the denial of all reality save that of one's own creation. It was Stevens' hope that the weapons of the realist (of those who see "things as they are") could be employed by the poet, that poetry could become part of reality, not merely an evasion of it. Thus his eventual dissatisfaction with the hieratic, with the spontaneous but ineffectual music of the oriole; thus his ambition to cross oriole with crow:

> *From oriole to crow, note the decline*
> *In music. Crow is realist. But, then*
> *Oriole, also, may be realist.*[83]

Yet, in spite of his heroic efforts at cross-breeding, Stevens remained too much the poet of negative capabilities to find in this genetic optimism that which will suffice. Unfortunately, the doctrine of oriole as realist declines with his music, and with an absurd logic that might have delighted Camus, the poet is forced back to his initial, half-skeptical view of poetry as

> *. . . a finikin thing of air*
> *That lives uncertainly and not for long*
> *Yet radiantly beyond much lustier blurs.*
>
> *For all his purple, the purple bird must have*
> *Notes for his comfort that he may repeat*
> *Through the gross tedium of being rare.*[84]

These comforting notes sing certainty, whose lack becomes a constant theme. If poetry is merely that "finikin thing of air," if it does not, for all its radiance, illuminate a reality outside itself, a new Peacockian question, as latent with menace as the Sphinx's riddle, cries for an answer:

> *Is the function of the poet here mere sound,*
> *Subtler than the ornatest prophecy,*
> *To stuff the ear?*[85]

The most sympathetic businessman could grant no more than this, and the quest for that which will suffice became for Stevens an agonizing dialogue between *hic* and *ille*, between Alastor and Mercutio, between oriole and crow. Some of the more practical effects of these tensions we have already observed in Stevens' erratic reticence to publish and, during two long periods, even to write. These reticences, it now seems safe to suggest, reflect that ambivalence toward poetry which we have described. More to our purpose, however, are the effects of this constant debate on Stevens' work itself, and particularly on the work of the *Harmonium* period, where whimsy and apparent nonsense are likely to stand most militantly opposed to our understanding.

III

The Two Voices:
Irony and Romance

WHEN A POET ATTEMPTS simultaneously to maintain two opposing attitudes, the resulting strain will force him into the precarious posture of irony, that manner of poetic address which makes it most nearly possible for him to express such attitudes without reconciling them. Detractors of the ironic method may, as Hugh Kenner suggests, regard it as a kind of jejune cynicism, "a pretext for fondling sentiment while depising it."[1] Yet, although there is certainly something of this perverse fondness for fouling what we love and loving what we foul in the modern ironist's method, the perversion is less the product of cynicism than of the desire for poetic sentiment sufficiently tough for our violent age. For better and for worse, it has been the plight of the modern poet to avoid the direct, the unambiguous, the "pure," and to strive for the oblique, the ambiguous, the "impure." As Robert Penn Warren has argued, modern taste requires that the obscenely cynical Mercutio be stationed outside the garden of love; the voices of the lovers are somehow more appealing to us, or at least more convincing, when we hear them against the counterpoint of our own cynicism. "Poetry wants to be pure," Warren writes, "but poems do not."[2]

To apply these observations to Stevens is to discover that the oriole wants to be pure, the crow does not. If Stevens' irony is frequently more strained and more facetious than that of his contemporaries, this is because the attraction of the pure, even of the "romantic," was stronger in him, and therefore the battle between oriole and crow the more violent. At its most characteristic, however, Stevens' irony is not simply a means of keeping poetic sentiment at a distance, like a poor relation with whom one would rather not seem to be acquainted; instead, it is from the poet himself that the poet stands aloof. Poet as subject views poet as object with faintly veiled distaste, no less marked because it is witty and indulgent. And, just as poet as object comes to resemble that arch-aesthete, Skimpole, whose fervid commitments to childish irresponsibility and to art for art's sake seemed equally ridiculous to the Dickens of *Bleak House,* so poetry itself is reduced to embroidery—again we recall Peacock—no more meaningful than "Floral Decorations for Bananas."[3]

The figure of the somewhat ridiculous poet engaged in a somewhat ridiculous pursuit appears most commonly in the work of the *Harmonium* period, when Stevens' relations with his own art were particularly strained.[4] The most obvious internal register of Stevens' ambivalence toward his poetry are the titles of the work he published from 1914 to 1923. "Peter Parasol," earlier discarded as a pseudonym, in 1919 became the title of a minor exercise which Stevens himself never reprinted.[5] The title, like "The Florist Wears Knee-Breeches,"[6] which he also left uncollected, harks back to the juvenile "Ballade of the Pink Parasol," being a quixotic sortie by foppish elegance against "This Vast Inelegance"[7] which Stevens challenged in another minor poem of this period.[8]

Were this particular ironic device confined to admitted trifles, we could better understand the subtly self-deprecatory attitude it seems intended to imply. However, we find similarly ironic titles affixed to many of Stevens' most ambitious early works. The figure of the poet as clown is evoked not only by "The Comedian as the Letter C," which deliberately employs a quasi-comic mode, but also by "Peter Quince at the Clavier" (or Wallace Stevens at the Harmonium), which does not.[9] To another, highly serious, virtuoso piece of the early period Stevens gave the title "Le Monocle de Mon Oncle," and here again the painfully self-conscious wit is out of keeping with the spirit of the poem. Although we may find amusing the ostentatious use of singsong schoolbook French—Stevens' own French, of course, was excellent—or the comic figure of the artist dandy (or possibly Apollo himself) whose monocle (art) keeps reality at one remove, we are nevertheless puzzled by the motive for this particular metaphor, which seems an attempt to deny responsibility for the poem that follows it, much in the same way as a serious novelist might try to explain away a bad book by remarking that he needed the money. In the same vein, but more harshly self-critical, is the title "Pecksniffiana," which Stevens assigned to a group of fourteen poems published in the October 1919 number of *Poetry*. Included in the group were such vintage pieces as "Fabliau of Florida," "The Weeping Burgher," "Anecdote of the Jar," and "The Paltry Nude Starts on a Spring Voyage";[10] yet here again Stevens appears to display ironic contempt for lyrics he considered trifling yet somehow brought himself to publish.

Less directly masochistic smacks at the poet as pretentious buffoon resound in such titles as "The Plot Against the Giant" and "Metaphors of a Magnifico," each of which, in conjunction with the poems they head, presents the artist as one who, either through sensuality or nihilistic solipsism, makes himself somewhat ridiculous by taking his art too seriously.[11] In a similar fashion, the title "Anecdote of the Prince of Peacocks" reduces the poet to a vain and gaudy subject for indulgent mockery.

Just as the titles we have already examined bring the artist under ironic scrutiny, others perform a similar operation on the poems beneath them. One of the less apparent illustrations of this kind of self-criticism is Stevens' fondness for the word "anecdote" in titles of this period. In the context we have established, it would appear that Stevens used the word to convey what, etymologically, is its "proper" meaning—in Skeats's definition: "an unpublished story," "a piece of gossip among friends."[12] Both senses serve the purpose of suggesting that these "anecdotal" poems are parables, cryptic little talks which have a secret meaning only for the initiates of the imagination. In this sense, the Susanna sections of "Peter Quince at the Clavier" constitute an anecdote. A far harsher, and far more elusive, titular self-indictment is "Gubbinal," toward whose root the *NED* can take us no closer than gubbins, a versatile noun which denotes, among other things, "fragments, especially of fish." Part of the joke, of course, is on us, but there remains that other part which allows the poet to draw a private analogy between his lyrics and fish-scraps.

The poem "Gubbinal" first appeared with eleven others under the group title "Sur Ma Guzzla Gracile,"[13] and here once more Stevens made game of his own ostentatious multilingualism. Toward the meaning of the elusive word, *guzzla,* we must again stop short of certainty, although not of probability. The Spanish *guzla* [sic] is a kind of one-string rebec, and this choice of an archaic instrument of rigidly limited range is not only characteristic of the ironic method we have been examining, but also foreshadows the most familiar of Stevens' titular ambiguities, "Harmonium" itself. The range of suggestion offered by this more versatile instrument has already been indicated, astutely and with gusto, although with perhaps too little attention to implicit self-mockery, by Lloyd Frankenberg:

> *Harmonium* perfectly conveys the scale, range of intensities, and formality of Wallace Stevens' early poems. A household instrument, rather outmoded, the harmonium was associated with the parlor, the "best" part of the house, often kept shut except on Sundays and special occasions. Stevens, an insurance salesman, was writing in his spare time, the "best" part of the day.
>
> More modestly volumed, the harmonium can simulate the grand tones of an organ and yet remain intimate, appropriate to family hymns [or, perhaps, to "anecdotes"]. Never Miltonic, their cultivated crescendos employ the harmonium's several stops for imitating woodwinds, brasses, and stringed instruments. . . . Most appropriate, the harmonium is an instrument that depends on breath; on alternate respirations.[14]

Frankenberg's respiratory allusion carries him neatly into a discussion of the pattern of alternation that informs "Earthy Anecdote," the opening poem of *Harmonium.* For our purpose, however, the bellows which supply air necessary for the harmonium's tones point

more appropriately "To the Roaring Wind," which
closes the volume:

> *What syllable are you seeking,*
> *Vocalissimus,*
> *In the distances of sleep?*
> *Speak it.*

"When we have gone all through Mr. Stevens,"
Edmund Wilson complained in 1924, "we find ourselves putting to him the same question that he himself
put to *The Roaring Wind.*"[15] Today, when we have
with time in fact gone all through Mr. Stevens, we
may understand more clearly that Stevens was relentless
in putting to himself most of the questions his critics
subsequently put to him; and of these questions, none
bears so directly on our case as those which Wilson
himself raised in the closing chapter of *Axel's Castle*:

> I believe . . . that the time is at hand when
> these writers who have largely dominated the liter-
> ary world of the decade 1920–30, though we shall
> continue to admire them as masters, will no longer
> serve us as guides. Axel's world of the private imagi-
> nation in isolation from the life of society seems
> to have been exploited and explored as far as for the
> present is possible. Who can imagine this sort of
> thing being carried further than Valéry and Proust
> have done? And who hereafter will be content to
> inhabit a corner, though fitted out with some
> things of one's own, in the shuttered house of one
> of these writers—where we find ourselves, also, be-
> coming conscious of lack of ventilation? On the
> other hand, it seems equally unsatisfactory, equally
> impossible, to imitate Rimbaud: we carry with us
> in our minds and habits the civilization of machin-
> ery, trade, democratic education and standardiza-

tion to the Africas and Asias to which we flee, even if we do not find them there before us. . . . The question begins to press us again as to whether it is possible to make a practical success of human society, and whether, if we continue to fail, a few masterpieces, however profound or noble, will be able to make life worth living even for the few people in a position to enjoy them.[16]

We shall discover that by the end of the period we have been examining, Stevens himself had found Axel's course and Rimbaud's at least temporarily closed to him. As an inhabitant of that "shuttered mansion-house" of which he spoke in "A Postcard from the Volcano," he too had suffered from lack of ventilation—indeed, had been temporarily suffocated by it. He too had sought refuge in several forms of primitivism, and had found Rimbaud's way finally unsatisfactory. In *Harmonium,* he had explored the aestheticism of Proust and Rimbaud to its outer borders. When, during the same period that Wilson was writing *Axel's Castle,* Stevens returned to poetry, he was prepared to encounter "the slime of men in crowds."[17]

II

If Wallace Stevens was a poet of vacillations, even of contradictions, the essential question on which his mind at times floundered was that same "perpetual question of unhappy humanity" that tormented Freud as it had tormented Bunyan: "What shall man do to be saved?" For Stevens as for Freud, salvation is equivalent to our capacity for temporal happiness; and for the poet as for the psychologist, the alternatives within whose extremes an answer could be sought were either: "Grow up and give up your infantile dreams of pleasure, recognize reality for what it is," or "Change this harsh reality so that you may recover lost sources of pleasure." In the Freudian terminology, these choices are between the reality-principle and the pleasure-principle. In Stevens' terms, they are between "realism" and "romanticism."[18]

Although Stevens frequently uses the term "romantic" and its variants in both his poetry and prose, he employs the term, as most of us do, in a variety of senses, at times with pejorative, at times with approbative, value.[19] Stevens himself never offers any very useful definition of "romantic," but I believe we can clarify his sense of the word, as well as the attitudes implicit in it for him, by examining the definitions offered by Ernst Cassirer and by Wyndham Lewis. According to Cassirer, whose analysis of romanticism Stevens quotes in the essay "Imagination as Value," one mark of romantic thought is the value placed upon imagination as against reason: "Imagination is no longer that special human activity which builds up the human world of art. It now has universal metaphysical value. Poetic imagination is the only clue to reality."[20] Cassirer, then, sees romantic thought as the product of an age of uncertainty, in which objective reality can no longer be rationally determined. Wyndham Lewis' definition only appears to contradict Cassirer's: the romantic, writes Lewis, *is the opposite of the real.* Romance is a thing that is in some sense non-existent. For instance, 'romance' is the reality of yesterday, or of tomorrow; or it is the reality of somewhere else. Romance is the great traditional enemy of the Present."[21] If for Cassirer romantic thought expresses dissatisfaction with conventional, rational modes of *knowing,* for Lewis it expresses dissatisfaction with conventional modes of *being*—that is, with the given contemporary reality to which prudence and reason ask us to adjust.

Stevens was defensive about his own fascination with the romantic, which, he once remarked, "looks like something completely contemptible in the light of literary intellectualism and cynicism."[22] Yet the concept of the romantic, as I have used Cassirer and Lewis to define it, had two irresistible attractions for him. Adherence to romantic thought in Cassirer's sense provided a comprehensive rationale for poetry by insisting that the poetic imagination, rather than denying reality, "is the only clue to reality." And romantic thought in Lewis' sense provided a means of resisting, or, if we will, escaping from a *present* reality that Stevens, like most men and all poets, found inadequate or hostile to the demands his imagination made on it. These two appeals are contradictory, I suggest, only if one insists that reality, at any given time, consists only of the empirically verifiable present. Yet such a concept of reality is unsatisfactory not only to the poet but also, I should expect, to the historian. The tragedy of an Adolph Eichmann, as Hannah Arendt has brilliantly argued, is precisely the result of the failure on the part of Eichmann and most of his compatriots to conceive of a reality beyond the nightmare present.[23]

Thus, when Stevens remarks that "the whole effort of the imagination is toward the production of the romantic,"[24] he is urging in effect that, through its enhancement of present reality, the work of art provides a vision of potential reality toward which the present material reality may aspire. This is one of the ways that art may aid us to recover lost sources of pleasure; and if, while reality is characteristically violent, such sources may be tapped only in the privacy of the individual aesthetic experience,[25] it is precisely that experience that teaches us to seek, and hopefully to find, the same sources of pleasure in the objective world around us. The essence of romanticism in this most radical sense was expressed by Keats in his famous remark to Benjamin Bailey: "The Imagination may be compared to Adam's dream—he awoke and found it truth."[26]

The analogy between Stevens' aesthetic dilemma and Freud's psychological dilemma can now be extended. Stevens' southern world is, in its purest form, what Norman O. Brown has called "the ideal kingdom of pleasure," which art knows how to recover.[27] The northern world, on the contrary, is the harsh present reality which demands, if we are to adjust to it, that we "grow up and give up [our] infantile dreams of pleasure."[28] And finally, the synthesis toward which Stevens' dialectic, like Freud's, attempted to move was a reality-principle "which at bottom also seeks pleasure—although a delayed and diminished pleasure, one which is assured by its realization of fact, its relation to reality."[29]

It should at this point be easier to understand why Stevens could in 1951 insist that the effort of the imagination is toward the production of the romantic, although only two years earlier he had written that "we must somehow cleanse the imagination of the romantic."[30] Such apparently contradictory statements on "the romantic" pervade Stevens' work, and cannot be explained in terms of any consistently evolving attitude. The explanation is rather that Stevens used the term "romantic" in at least two sharply opposed senses. In the approbative sense which we have examined, romanticism means the art of aggrandizement, of envisioning a reality more adequate than the present state of empirical reality to the demands our imaginations make on it. Such visions may, to do paraphrastic violence to Lewis, be rooted in lost but recoverable values of the past or in potential values of the future. Stevens' fondness for the Caribbean and other exotic settings is simply one means of insisting on his awareness that the pleasures of the imagination which he experiences and records are not, properly, pleasures in harmony with our time and our place.

In the pejorative sense, the romantic "is to the imagination what sentimentality is to feeling. It is a failure of the imagination precisely as sentimentality is a failure of feeling."[31] The romantic in this sense is the enemy of the imagination, since the imagination "is intrepid and eager and the extreme of its achievement lies in abstraction. The achievement of the romantic, on the contrary, lies in minor wish-fulfillments and it is incapable of abstraction."[32] This kind of romanticism is negatively escapist; it is incapable of abstraction because it is based on subjective wish-fulfillments that reflect simply an inability to confront present reality, rather than wish-fulfillments rooted in full comprehension of that reality and suggesting, through projections of the imagination, the courses by which we may bring that reality to transcend itself.

It should now be possible to suggest some of the ways in which Stevens' concern with romantic theory and practice provide an approach to his poetry itself. First, the mode of self-mockery to which I called attention in the previous section can in part be understood as Stevens' reaction against his own concessions to what he sometimes called the "dead romantic"[33]—that is, against a poetry of wish-fulfillment not founded on realization of fact.[34] Second, the strenuous, even anguished attempt to confront the contemporary world of chaos and violence that particularly characterized Stevens' poetry in the thirties and during the period of the Second World War—this attempt reflects positively, as his self-mockery reflects negatively, Stevens' determination to explore the possibility of an art based on the reality-principle, on what Stevens called "things as they are." We have finally to mention Stevens' life-long—but in later years increasingly explicit—interest in the relationship between the imagination and reality. This interest did not seem to Stevens, as it does to Randall Jarrell, either extraneous or hostile to the writing of poetry; neither, for that matter, was it inspired by any mere "academic" interest in aesthetic theory. Rather, it was based on the convictions that "The theory of poetry is the life of poetry," that "The theory of poetry is the theory of life," and finally, most urgently, that "Reality is not what it is. It consists of the many realities which it can be made into."[35] As aesthetician, no less than poet, Stevens' fundamental concern was with tracing the implications of his tenet that "The purpose of poetry is to contribute to man's happiness";[36] and the nature of this contribution, he believed, was to revitalize without ignoring our present modes of experience, and to project, as the imagination alone allows us to project, visions of a rich and spiritually nourishing world in which man might come to live.

As I suggested at the beginning of this section, Stevens' art, like Freud's psychology, is dedicated to the task of human redemption, to the awakening of faculties, repressed or undeveloped, through which the individual and the society could achieve a degree of temporal happiness, and achieve it without ignoring or in any way disguising what to both poet and psychologist were the *facts* of human mortality and human independence from divine sponsorship. We must understand, therefore, that when Stevens gave to the final section of "Notes Toward a Supreme Fiction" the subtitle "It Must Give Pleasure," he was not subscribing to a conception of poetry like, for example, that of W. H. Auden, for whom poetry is a particularly sophisticated form of amusement. Stevens, on the contrary, shared with his romantic predecessors the belief that one of the functions of poetry is to make men poets. The poet's obligation, Stevens properly insists, is not in any ordinary sense "a social obligation"; the poet does not "lead people out of the confusion in which they find themselves," nor does he "comfort them while they follow their [leaders] to and fro."[37] The poet's obligation, qua poet, " is to make his imagination theirs, and . . . he fulfills himself only as he sees his imagination become the light in the minds of others. His role, in short, is to help people to live their lives."[38] On this point Stevens differs in only one respect from Wordsworth or Shelley: whereas the Romantics could still dream that poetry might perform this humanizing function for all men, Stevens is perforce resigned to the fact that the contemporary poet addresses himself to an elite. Since, however, the question of whether a serious poet addresses himself to an elite or to a mass audience is one that must ultimately be answered by the society and not by the poet, I do not believe that it must further engage us here.

What should engage us is this quite different question: if the poet helps men to live their lives by making them, in effect, poets themselves, what are the rewards men are to enjoy by becoming poets? Obviously Stevens does not mean that when the poet's imagination becomes the imagination of his readers, his readers will necessarily begin to write poems. He is concerned rather with the possibility of creating readers who can perceive and feel as a poet perceives and feels, and to the extent that he succeeds in creating them, poetry may come to serve the public function once served by religion.[39] Ideally, such readers will learn to inhabit, if only on occasion, a world of poetry indistinguishable from the world in which we live, or, I ought to say . . . in which we shall come to live, since what makes the poet the potent figure he is, or was, or ought to be, is that he creates the world to which we turn incessantly and without knowing it and that he gives to life the supreme fictions without which it is impossible to conceive it.[40]

But basic to this lofty function is a more simple one: poetry gives "a sense of the freshness or vividness of life."[41]

Although the pleasure to be derived from this sense of freshness is ultimately more than sensual, it has sensual pleasure at its root, the kind of pleasure experienced by Bonnie and Josie, dancing around a stump in Oklahoma, when they cry: " 'Ohoyaho,/ Ohoo' . . ./ Celebrating the marriage/ Of flesh and air."[42] Critics like Yvor Winters, who attack Stevens on the ground of his hedonism, are at bottom expressing their Malvolian discomfort over a poetry whose function is the enhancement of pleasure, a poetry explicitly dedicated to the premise that "A poet looks at the world as a man looks at a woman."[43]

The most intense sensual pleasure is the sexual experience, and the poet's response to the beauty of the world is in several ways analogous to a man's response to the beauty of a woman. Both responses are sensual at bottom, and both seek union with the object of beauty, one through an act of imaginative love that we call crudely "the aesthetic experience," and the other through the act of physical love. That Stevens, like Theseus, held the lover and the poet "to be of imagination all compact" can be observed through his frequent use of the marriage ceremony as metaphor for the establishment of harmony between man and his environment,[44] and through his even more frequent use of woman as metaphor for the beauty of the earth. The analogy also explains why it is difficult to say of a poem like "Le Monocle de Mon Oncle" whether it is a celebration of love or art; in fact it is simultaneously a celebration of both. For our present purpose, however, "Peter Quince at the Clavier"[45] offers the most fruitful illustration of the complex interrelationships between sexual and aesthetic experience. Published in 1915, several months earlier than "Sunday Morning," "Peter Quince" was only the third poem of the *Harmonium* period to reach print, and it is the first poem of fundamental importance that Stevens published. It may thus be examined as Stevens' point of poetic departure, and as the point to which all of his subsequent poetic voyages aspired to return.

"Peter Quince" develops in a pattern of continually expanding and intricately interwoven analogies, according to a process that can be studied in simpler form in the short lyric "The Load of Sugar-Cane."[46] The poem opens with a definition of the beauty of art as existing not as a thing in itself; its reality consists not in its physical medium, but in its effect on its audience. By choosing the pianist as token of the artist, Stevens is able to combine in a single figure the artist and his audience, to suggest the identity between the two, and thus to illustrate the manner in which the artist makes his imagination *that of* his audience. The movement of the opening three lines is thus circular: just as the fingers of the pianist on the keyboard produce music as sound, so he, reciprocally, becomes instrument when his emotions are played upon by music. This second, "true" music of feeling now becomes the subject for further definition by analogy: if music is feeling, then feeling is music;

and the pianist's sensual desire for the woman dressed in "blue-shadowed silk" to whom his thoughts now turn is music too.

In fewer than eight lines Stevens has developed a complex statement on the reciprocal relations between art and feeling, music and sensual desire; from this point onward it will be impossible to say that the primary interest of the poem is either art *or* desire, for the two have become inextricably fused. Thus the Susanna motif, which occupies the body of the poem, is not simply an illustration of the relatively abstract idea already established. Although it is introduced as a simile for "what I feel,/ Here in this room, desiring you," it is in fact a concrete embodiment of the entire statement of the opening lines; it is what Stevens has called "an abstraction blooded," without which we would not experience the true poem, the poem of feeling. Simultaneously, then, Susanna is both the particular woman whom "Peter Quince" desires and the more general beauty that inspires feeling and leads to the creation of art. Similarly, the lustful elders (Stevens, at thirty-six, was no longer a youthful lover) are identified with "Peter Quince" both through the sexual desire they share with him and through their more abstract role as pursuers of beauty. In brief, Susanna is *a* woman and Beauty; the elders are lustful men, and artists.

Linking the Susanna section of the poem to the frame, the elders' lust is music, a "strain" wakened in them by the bathing girl, the sight of whom makes

> *The basses of their beings throb*
> *In witching chords, and their thin blood*
> *Pulse pizzicati of Hosanna.*

That the music Susanna evokes should take the form of religious praise is appropriate not only in terms of the elders' historical role. Just as the account of the elders' desire echoes the introductory lines, so it foreshadows the poem's close: our response to beauty constitutes a *"sacrament* of praise" as aesthetics begins to appropriate the language of religion. In our own age of unbelief, Stevens could hope, art might eventually come to provide all the satisfactions once provided by a belief in God.

The second section of the poem is, like the first, governed by the analogy between feeling and music. Susanna's own languorous imaginings are melody, but gentle, in contrast with the throbbing music of the elders. What Susanna experiences at her bath is, essentially, a perfect unity with the natural world, of which she is able to feel herself a part. In the water's caresses, she finds "concealed imaginings," and her sense of identity with her environment is, like the elders' longing for her, a sexual experience, but consummated as theirs is not. Risen from her bath,

> *Upon the bank, she stood*
> *In the cool*
> *Of spent emotions.*
> *She felt, among the leaves,*
> *The dew of old devotions.*

As *a* woman, Susanna's emotions are characterized by a narcissism that Freud finds characteristic of the normal erotic attitudes of woman.[47] As a personification of the world of beauty and pleasure that art aspires to recover, Susanna enjoys a timelessness, a self-dependence, an alienation from human modes of relationship—qualities that throughout Stevens' work characterize the objective physical beauty that art pursues but can never wholly capture. At the moment when the cymbals' crash and roaring horns announce the elders' intrusion and attempt to consummate their desire for her, Susanna's perfection and self-containment are broken, and she stands naked and ashamed. The elders' experience is thus analogous to the artist's, whose attempt to capture beauty as a *ding an sich* can result only in a momentary glimpse (or at best in an imitation of) the self-contained perfection of his subject. Objective physical beauty eludes his art in the same way that the blackbird eludes the poet's thirteen attempts to capture it.

Quite obviously, then, the elders' attempt to ravish Susanna is not for Stevens, as it was for the apocryphal writer, a moral fact ("ethics," as Stevens puts it elsewhere, "are no more a part of poetry than they are of painting"[48]) but rather an aesthetic fact, a dramatized statement of the paradoxical argument with which the fourth and final section of the poem begins:

> *Beauty is momentary in the mind—*
> *The fitful tracing of a portal;*
> *But in the flesh it is immortal.*

This deliberate inversion of Platonic aesthetics leads, finally, to the poem's ultimate claim: that art, the religion of beauty, may provide us with the comfort of an immortality more satisfactory, because rooted in reality, than any paradise-centered religion can provide. In "Sunday Morning" the perennial return of April's green becomes, through its reality, a more solid ground for "imperishable bliss" than the heavens men invent to satisfy their desire for permanence; in "Peter Quince" the continual rebirth of the beauty Susanna embodied— manifest in the recurrence of natural as well as human forms—becomes, despite its continual death in nature and in man, the object of our worship in the religion of earth.

Even in "Peter Quince," however, which embodies

in itself some of the noblest sanctions that can be claimed for high art and high artists, Stevens remains responsive to the artist's ironic, even tragic role, and it is this awareness of disparity between the artist's aspiration and what in reality he can achieve that accounts for the self-mockery of the poem's title. As "Susanna's music touched the bawdy strings/ Of those white elders," so is the poet's music "bawdy" by comparison with the chords it seeks to echo. Continually awakened by his desire for immortal beauty and continually left with "only Death's ironic scraping," the poet takes comfort finally in the music of feeling, not sound, that Susanna embodied and evokes:

> *Now, in its immortality, it plays*
> *On the clear viol of her memory,*
> *And makes a constant sacrament of praise.*

In the end, as "bawdy strings" are transformed into "clear viol," Stevens accomplishes through art precisely what his poem argues art cannot accomplish.

"Peter Quince" is Stevens' earliest attempt to present the ideal and timeless "kingdom of pleasure which art knows how to recover"; yet even here, in one of his least qualified celebrations of the pleasure-principle, the obstacles that oppose man's attempt to wed himself to beauty are as essential to the poem as the celebration of that beauty itself. Like Keats, Stevens is aware that the ultimate perfection of art can be achieved only through a stasis that is irreconcilable with life. Keats's urn is a "cold pastoral," just as Susanna, without the elders, is alien to man, and characterized by, even identified with, the inhuman self-containment and timelessness of nature. Poetry wants to be pure; the poem does not. If poetry seeks, on the one hand, to transcend man's imperfect, time-bound state, to achieve the timelessness of Keats's bright star, Blake's Beulah, or Yeats's golden bird, the poet remains aware that such perfection can be achieved only in death, that indeed it is a kind of death. The artist, if he is to remain an artist, must respond to the tensions between timeless pleasure toward which art aspires and the mortality and flux on which life insists. Like Stevens' Crispin, he will conceive his voyaging to be

> *An up and down between two elements,*
> *A fluctuating between sun and moon,*
> *A sally into gold and crimson forms,*
> *As on this voyage, out of goblinry,*
> *And then retirement like a turning back*
> *And sinking down to the indulgences*
> *That in the moonlight have their habitude.*[49]

It is this fluctuating between sun and moon, between the world of is and the world of ought to be, between the reality-principle and the pleasure-principle, that provide the basic pattern of Stevens' work.

IV

Adam's Dream

WE HAVE ALREADY observed that for Stevens the poetic pursuit of pleasure was among the most urgent tasks in which a twentieth-century poet could engage. The poetic enactment of pleasure is, after all, equivalent to what Irving Howe has properly argued to be the main concern of Stevens' poetry: "discovering and . . . enacting the possibilities for human self-renewal in an impersonal and recalcitrant age."[1] This enactment, as we have seen in our examination of "Peter Quince at the Clavier," requires that we maintain our capacity for imaginative, even amatory, response to physical beauty, and from it learn modes of subjective experience worthy of mirroring the external world that feeds the spirit. Stevens' boldest and most famous attempt to embody this process is "Sunday Morning," a poem in which the natural beauty earlier symbolized by Susanna is confronted nakedly as explicit subject. And the poem may properly be called "romantic," not only in the special sense I have discussed, but also because it celebrates, in blank verse that rivals and in some particulars may have been influenced by Wordsworth's own,[2] a physical world sufficient to satisfy those instincts for order, certainty, and comfort which in former times were satisfied by the idea of God.

In his essay on "The Irrational Element in Poetry," Stevens was later to remark:

> while it can lie in the temperament of very few of us to write poetry in order to find God, it is probably the purpose of each of us to find the good which, in the Platonic sense, is synonymous with God. One writes poetry, then, in order to approach the good in what is harmonious and orderly.[3]

The statement, like nearly all of Stevens' prose meditations, is an attempt to make explicit the theory that governed his poetry from the start; and together with his remark that "the great poems of heaven and hell have been written and the great poem of the earth remains to be written,"[4] it provides a frame for Stevens' own great poem of the earth. It may be that Stevens nowhere comes closer than in "Sunday Morning" to "enacting the possibilities for human self-renewal." It is certain that here, in a poem that was composed so early in his poetic career, Stevens has already created one of those major works that were to recur throughout his canon: a poem shaped in the image of the Supreme Fiction, looming over the lesser lyrics that surround it like that magical tree of reality in "Le Monocle de Mon Oncle," which

> . . . *stands gigantic, with a certain tip*
> *To which all birds come sometime in their time.*
> *But when they go that tip still tips the tree.*[5]

As usual with Stevens' work, the title provides a complex gloss on the poem that follows it; and those who have considered Stevens' titles either merely frivolous or somehow irrelevant to his texts have missed one of the widest portals into his rich world. Sunday, of course, is a day of meditation particularly important to Stevens, who could play his harmonium only during such spare moments as his quotidian responsibilities might allow. The day is also God's day, and the poem is concerned with prescribing the manner of celebrating God—or rather, what "a God might be"—in the modern world. The importance of this point can hardly be exaggerated, since for Stevens, no less than for Matthew Arnold, the salient function of art was one we may legitimately call a religious function. As Stevens put it in the "Adagia,"

> The relation of art to life is of the first importance especially in a skeptical age since, in the absence of a belief in God, the mind turns to its own creations and examines them, not alone from the aesthetic point of view, but for what they reveal, for what they validate and invalidate, for the support that they give.[6]

It was Stevens' conviction that although we can, if only because we must, learn to live without God, we cannot, if we are to remain human, live without the satisfactions that belief in God could formerly provide. Whatever else religion of more devout ages than our own may have done, it did at least supply substance for visions grander than the empiricism of the present age has been able to achieve; and although Stevens seems never to have suffered anguish over the loss of God, he did consider it the burden and the privilege of the poet to rescue from that loss values which man requires and may attain even without God.

On another, less obvious but equally important level, the title reminds us that Sunday is the day of the sun, and that the sun has quite logically been considered in most primitive societies to be the life-giver, the emblem of fertility and procreation. If "Sunday Morning" is a celebration of life, a hymn to things as they are, it is also a poem of potential and renewal, a sermon on things as they might be, an instance of that "world of poetry indistinguishable from the world in which we live, or . . . from the world in which we shall come to live."[7] And finally, as Stevens was later to write, "poetry is like prayer in that it is most effective in solitude and in times of solitude, as, for example, in the earliest morning."[8]

"Sunday Morning," then, is a visionary poem; indeed, we might call it the ultimate projection of the romantic vision into the twentieth century. The importance of "Sunday Morning" to Stevens' subsequent poetry is that, although he would never again find it possible to pay, without irony and without qualification, such exultant homage to the sun, "symbol of the good which . . . is synonymous with God," the remainder of his work would nevertheless be devoted to the attempt, at times comic, at times ironic, at times heroically triumphant, to create a poetry of exaltation, yet a poetry which is, as he came to think the work of the *Harmonium* period was not, attuned to modern reality. It is Stevens' faith in the possibility of making poetry out of the world as seen in the clear light of reality, out of the Platonic sun that is the source of all knowledge and all truth—the possibility of metamorphosing, somehow without distortion, things as they palpably are into things as the imagination wills them to be—that is the solid core of his most lofty aspiration.

Although the structure of "Sunday Morning" takes the loose shape of meditation and association, not the rigid form of logic, its pattern of thought and feeling, unlike that of many of Stevens' meditative poems, does move toward resolution. The female protagonist[9] suffers at the start the quiet unrest which loss of those consolations attainable through faith in Christ has stirred in her; in the course of the subsequent dialogue between her longings for "some imperishable bliss" and the poet's assurances that transience is all and is enough, she is drawn from religious yearnings to an acceptance of a world without God. Thus, when with the closing image of "casual flocks of pigeons" which, at evening, make

> *Ambiguous undulations as they sink,*
> *Downward to darkness, on extended wings,*

the fact of death is again brought into the foreground, it is no longer a source of terror or unrest, nor does it inspire religious intimations of immortality; now "Death is the mother of beauty," and, as in Keats, through acceptance of earthly transience we are wedded most passionately to the beauty we are certain we must lose.

How may we refine from earth itself sufficient compensation for that "imperishable bliss" promised by heaven? The process begins subtly before the argument of the poem is engaged. Here is one of the few poems by Stevens in which there is no obvious reference, either direct or metaphoric, to poetry itself; yet the opening stanza serves brilliantly to illustrate what in "Three Academic Pieces" Stevens argues to be the singular quality that elevates poetry above other pleasurable things: poetry, he argues there, by revealing "a partial similarity between dissimilar things," intensifies and makes more brilliant the particular element of their similarity. "When the similarity is between things of adequate dignity," he goes on,

> the resemblance may be said to transfigure or sublimate them. Take, for example, the resemblance between reality and any projection of it in belief or in metaphor. What is it that these two have in

common? Is not the glory of the idea of any future state a relation between a present and a future glory? The brilliance of the earth is the brilliance of every paradise.[10]

Just as the two closing sentences of this passage constitute a prose summary of one of the central themes of "Sunday Morning," so the argument that precedes them serves to explain the method of the opening stanza. The lady is neither a person nor even a *persona;* she is simply the projection of a mood which, were it to take on a palpable being of its own, would resemble the feminine image Stevens here projects. It should not surprise us, then, if beneath the lady's peignoir we find no flesh. Similarly, her rich ambience is designed not so much to provide "real toads in imaginary gardens" as to foreshadow the imaginative aggrandizement of the material world through which we may come to see that "The brilliance of the earth is the brilliance of every paradise."

The associative richness of the opening stanza is nearly inexhaustible, and within it reality and its metaphoric projection become nearly inseparable. The coffee, oranges, and cockatoo, which at first, as sensual comforts and tokens of a luxuriant mood,

> . . . *mingle to dissipate*
> *The holy hush of ancient sacrifice,*

become, as the lady's imagination weaves them into dream, into poetry, "things in some procession of the dead," a procession in which the dreamer herself, as if enchanged by her own images, finds herself taking part:

> *The day is like wide water, without sound,*
> *Stilled for the passing of her dreaming feet*
> *Over the seas, to silent Palestine,*
> *Dominion of the blood and sepulchre.*

All roads in the first stanza lead to Palestine, to the lady's meditations on Christ; she, like the earthly riches that surround her, is in reality a thing "in some procession of the dead," for she is mortal; "the pungent oranges and bright green wings" of the cockatoo become, through their tropical associations, fit imaginative companions for her southern journey; and finally, the similarity between the gentle violation of her somnolent mood by thoughts of the Crucifixion ("the dark/ Encroachment of that old catastrophe") and the almost imperceptible manner in which "a calm darkens among water lights," leads her thoughts to Palestine as silently and as surely as Christ himself walked upon the water.[11]

What has occurred in the first stanza is that, in constructing her metaphysical poem, the lady has given "her bounty to the dead." Indeed, her creative act is precisely the kind later rejected by Crispin, "that poetic hero without palms/ Or jugglery," whose

> . . . *violence was for aggrandizement*
> *And not for stupor, such as music makes*
> *For sleepers halfway waking.*[12]

The lady's imagination and her heart's need having filled her mind with "the holy hush of ancient sacrifice," the second voice, as gentle as the movement of her mind, yet less passive, less feminine, is introduced. Its argument is untouched by any skepticism against her need, but is rather concerned with establishing an alternate solace to the religious comfort she has sought in Christ. And its opening question provides what is at once a delicately articulated transition and an example of Stevens' most subtle wit:

> *Why should she give her bounty to the dead?*
> *What is divinity if it can come*
> *Only in silent shadows and in dreams?*

> *Shall she not find in comforts of the sun,*
> *In pungent fruit and bright green wings, or else*
> *In any balm or beauty of the earth*
> *Things to be cherished like the thought of heaven?*

The fruit, the wings, initially synecdoches for "the balm or beauty of the earth," transported her from their own reality to another balm, the balm of heaven. Yet that more orthodox comforting, although itself mothered by the imagination, depends, as it has always done, on the denial of the poem of earth. The earth, from whose substance we have woven our visionary paradises, is paradise enough to those with sufficient feeling to be *alive* in it.

In an era whose intense self-consciousness has led to an ever-widening alienation from the objective world, Stevens, who is at times the most solipsistic of modern poets, returned in "Sunday Morning" to Coleridge's concept of the "One Life," a poetic and epistemological state to be entered only when "A poet's heart and intellect [are] combined and unified with the great appearances of nature and not merely held in solution and loose mixture with them, in the shape of formal similes." Our divinity consists in an awareness of the "One Life," in our capacity, as Stevens puts it elsewhere, for "Celebrating the marriage/ Of flesh and air,"[13] not a marriage of man and God but one whose rituals are celebrated in the closing lines of the second stanza—a marriage of the human and divine within man, to be consummated through an imaginative capacity to unite ourselves with the earth:

> *Divinity must live within herself:*
> *Passions of rain, or moods in falling snow;*
> *Grieving in loneliness, or unsubdued*
> *Elations when the forest blooms; gusty*

Emotions on wet roads on autumn nights;
All pleasures and all pains, remembering
The bough of summer and the winter branch.
These are the measures destined for her soul.

As the second stanza rejects the shadowy bliss of
heaven for the certain pleasures (and the certain pains)
of earth, the third elaborates the Blakean motto: "All
deities reside in the human breast." Just as our emotions
may unite us with the paradise of earth, so may the
imaginative power with which we created the gods fit us
with the requisite dignity to live in this paradise.[14] The
argument of the stanza becomes clear enough when we
realize that Stevens is in effect quoting scripture to his
purpose. The concept of divinity, here emblemized by
Jove, becomes a fruitful concept only *after* men have
created myths that wed the human to the divine. These
myths, conceived out of our hunger for divine magnificence, for breaching the gap between the real and the
ideal, comprise, as Stevens knew with Blake, our earliest
poetry; born out of longing for the superhuman, these
myths conceived in their turn new symbols of human
superhumanity, emblemized by the constellations in
which Jove's discarded mistresses achieved immortality.
Although Stevens confines his argument to classical
mythology, the analogy with Christianity is apparent.
Christ, too, Stevens reminds us by implication, was
born out of our desire to commingle the human and divine; and in the Christian myth as in the pagan, the
success of that commingling was symbolized by a star.
In both cases, a god has come down to man, and man
has in turn been elevated to the heavens.

Stevens' treatment of these myths, it should be
apparent, is unmarked by either hostility or cynicism
toward religion. He sees religious myths rather as the

products of timeless human needs which must be satisfied in a post-religious era no less than in the earlier ages of faith. In short, we still require the transcendental imagination that went into the making of our gods, as it still goes into the making of our poetry. But in a naturalistic universe, the earth itself is the only paradise and the most proximate immortality we can know. Thus, lest "our blood fail," it is through a wedding of our blood to the earth that we can experience the contentment we once experienced in the hope of heaven:

> *The sky will be much friendlier then than now,*
> *A part of labor and a part of pain,*
> *And next in glory to enduring love,*
> *Not this dividing and indifferent blue.*

Through our recognition that the earth is "all of paradise that we shall know" we may come at last to be at home in it—this is the truth visible in the clear light of the sun; this is the attachment to life which for Stevens, as for Camus, only the acceptance of the finality of death can bring.

The dialogue does not end, however, with this lofty conception. The lady, who is not, after all, "A High-Toned Old Christian Woman" but a facet of Stevens' own mind, still demands some satisfaction for the fundamental theistic craving for permanence:

> *She says, "I am content when wakened birds,*
> *Before they fly, test the reality*
> *Of misty fields, by their sweet questionings;*
> *But when the birds are gone, and their warm fields*
> *Return no more, where, then, is paradise?"*

The answer is direct and its limpid rhetoric is persuasive: there is no visionary heaven

> . . . *that has endured*
> *As April's green endures; or will endure*
> *Like her remembrance of awakened birds,*
> *Or her desire for June and evening, tipped*
> *By the consummation of the swallow's wings.*

Once more the poetry of earth is pitted against that of heaven, and its superiority, Stevens insists, stems from its permanence *as* reality. We are reminded, although he would hardly rejoice in the context of our reminiscence, of Dr. Johnson's injunction to a bereaved friend:

> Let us endeavor to see things as they are, and then enquire whether we ought to complain. Whether to see life as it is will give us much consolation, I know not; but the consolation which is drawn from truth, if any there be, is solid and durable; that which may be derived from errour must be, like its original, falacious and fugitive.[15]

To say that the Keatsian fifth stanza is repetitive would be to miss the key fact of the poem's structure, for "Sunday Morning" is, like most of Stevens' longer poems, a set of variations on a theme. Indeed, the lady's final reiteration of the need expressed in the stanza's opening lines ("But in contentment I still feel/ The need of some imperishable bliss") illustrates a technique with which the reader of Stevens becomes increasingly familiar: it is a flat statement of what, in the opening lines of stanza four, was uttered in metaphor. Similarly, the lines that follow in the stanza offer a metaphor for the vision of earth as paradise that is parallel to the vision earlier embodied in the image of the wakened birds. Poetry, Stevens has said, is an "abstraction blooded," and it is clear enough that the abstraction here blooded is that "Death is the mother of beauty."

Not so clear, however, is the idea behind lines 13 and 14, in which death "causes boys to pile new plums and pears/ On disregarded plate." The intended meaning of these lines would indeed be impossible to determine with any confidence were it not for Harriet Monroe's objection to them when Stevens submitted the poem to her in 1915. "The words 'On disregarded plate' in No. 5," Stevens wrote to her in reply,

> are, apparently, obscure. Plate is used in the sense of so-called family plate. Disregarded refers to the disuse into which things fall that have been possessed for a long time. I mean, therefore, that death releases and renews. What the old have come to disregard, the young inherit and make use of. Used in these senses, the words have a value in the lines which I find difficult to retain in any change. Does this explanation help? Or can you make any suggestion? I ask this because your criticism is clearly well founded.
>
> The lines might read,
>
> She causes boys to bring sweet-smelling pears,
> And plums in ponderous piles. The maidens taste
> And stray etc.
>
> But such a change is somewhat pointless. I should prefer the lines unchanged, although, if you like the variations proposed, for the sake of clearness, I should be satisfied.[16]

Miss Monroe liked the variation proposed, and Stevens was satisfied,[17] although in the revised lines he indeed lost the value he originally intended. When we consider the weight of meaning Stevens himself piled on the "disregarded plate," meaning which no unaided reader could possibly taste, it should neither surprise nor dismay us that certain images and even certain poems throughout his work must remain obscure.

With the sixth stanza the current quickens as it carries the argument toward resolution. The permanence we pine for is the static permanence of death:

> *Is there no change of death in paradise?*
> *Does ripe fruit never fall? Or do the boughs*
> *Hang always heavy in that perfect sky,*
> *Unchanging, yet so like our perishing earth,*
> *With rivers like our own that seek for seas*
> *They never find, the same receding shores*
> *That never touch with inarticulate pang?*

A paradise in which all is consummated is a paradise without consummation; a paradise in which all desire is satisfied is a paradise of ennui:

> *Why set the pear upon those river banks*
> *Or spice the shores with odors of the plum?*[18]

We may break Stevens' argument down into three essential points: (1) The most radiant paradise we can conceive is one in which earth's brilliant beauty is perpetual—that is, a paradise in which neither nature nor man is subject to change and death. Essentially, this is the paradise Milton depicts in the prelapsarian Eden. (2) Precisely because the beauty of such a paradise *is* changeless and immortal, it would provide none of the emotional intensity that earthly beauty provides; for that intensity has its source in our awareness that earth's bounties are not ours forever. (3) By extension were we to enjoy, on earth *or* in heaven, that which we most passionately crave—"imperishable bliss"—we would, paradoxically, be robbed of bliss altogether, and be bound instead to the endless reexperiencing of pleasures that would become steadily more cloying through repetition.

Thus, with a cogency never achieved by Dr. Pangloss, Stevens completes his demonstration that this is indeed, the imminence of death notwithstanding, the best of all possible worlds. Nor is it difficult to imagine Stevens' reply to those dark lines of Yeats: "Man is in love and loves what vanishes,/ What more is there to say?" There remains to say, Stevens might have said, that if man were *not* in love with what vanishes, he would not be capable of loving at all. This, in effect, is the argument with which the stanza closes:

> *Death is the mother of beauty, mystical*
> *Within whose burning bosom we devise*
> *Our earthly mothers waiting, sleeplessly.*

Death mothers beauty because without awareness of death we would not learn the nurture of our earthly mother, the physical beauty of the world itself, a beauty that is "sleepless" and divine, unlike the hollow divinity that comes "Only in silent shadows and in dreams."

The seventh stanza of the poem might take for its motto Nietzsche's statement that "We have produced the hardest possible thought; now let us create the creature who will accept it lightheartedly and blissfully." The symbolic ceremony of devotion to the life-source that the stanza so grandly describes is not, as Yvor Winters would maintain, a projection of finicky hedonism, but rather an expression of faith in the possible heavenly fellowship of those Nietzschean creatures, "Of men that perish and of summer morn," of men content with the knowledge that

> *. . . whence they come and whither they shall go*
> *The dew upon their feet shall manifest.*

Nor would it seem a token of spiritual ennui that this poem in celebration of "an old chaos of the sun" should end with an evocation of death in life and life in death the nobility and scrupulous integrity of whose rhetoric requires no gloss:

> *Deer walk upon our mountains, and the quail*
> *Whistle about us their spontaneous cries;*
> *Sweet berries ripen in the wilderness;*
> *And, in the isolation of the sky,*
> *At evening, casual flocks of pigeons make*
> *Ambiguous undulations as they sink,*
> *Downward to darkness on extended wings.*

The cockatoo of the first stanza, the "green wings" of the second, the "wakened birds" of the fourth, achieve synthesis in the "casual flocks of pigeons" whose sinking undulations bring the poem to a close.[19] The lady *does*, in the end, give her bounty to the dead after all; not, however, as she had done initially, by sacrificing sensual experience to the falsifying hope of immortality, but by accepting transience as the necessary condition of our humanity and of our sense of beauty.

Skeptical, yet inspired by a passionate faith, contemporary, yet rooted in a primitive conception of the three-fold tie that binds nature, man, and divinity into an exultant harmony anomalous in an age that conceives "nature" as that which one beholds on picnics, and an age in which the idea of human potential for divinity has become repugnant to humanist and theist alike, "Sunday Morning" stands in the garden of contemporary poetry like some great exotic flowering tree transported into a municipal park by an eccentric millionaire.

Yet the fact remains that "Sunday Morning" *is* an exotic, whose beauty and whose power, as Stevens himself would shortly come to believe, had their nurture in a climate and an age remote from our own. Randall

Jarrell came close to recognizing this point when he remarked of the poem that in it "is the last purity and refinement of the grand style, as perfect, in its calm transparency, as the best of Wordsworth. . . ."[20] But for the achievement of that purity and refinement, Stevens was forced to pay a price. In "Sunday Morning" he does not, as he was later to say that the poet must, "move constantly in the direction of the credible."[21] That "ring of men" chanting in orgy "Their boisterous devotion to the sun" may stir us, but will not for long, even as metaphor, win from us a "willing suspension of disbelief." Moreover, Jarrell's reference to "the last purity and refinement of the grand style" is in itself, however unintentionally, but ambiguous praise: Stevens' richly articulated blank verse marks the *end* of a technical tradition, just as his insistence on our source in nature marks the end of a spiritual one. Stevens, like Picasso, began his mature artistic career with mastery of the received tradition; insofar as the vital artist is a pioneer, however, such mastery can bring stasis as leaden as that of a changeless paradise itself. To a degree, then, "Sunday Morning" is at once masterpiece and dead end; and our final response to the poem will be tempered by our recollection of Stevens' own subsequent remarks on Verrocchio's statue of Bartolommeo Colleoni:

> One feels the passion of rhetoric begin to stir and even to grow furious; and one thinks that, after all, the noble style, in whatever it creates, merely perpetuates the noble style. In this statue, the apposition between the imagination and reality is too favorable to the imagination.[22]

"Sunday Morning" is the point of embarkation for the aesthetic voyaging of Crispin, the poet-clown who was to be Stevens' most ambitious vehicle for self-satire.

Toward the close of his voyage, shortly before he abandons poetic theory and practice for domestic tranquility, Crispin turns against his own visions, visions of which "Sunday Morning" was the consummate embodiment:

> These bland excursions into time to come,
> Related in romance to backward flights,
> However prodigal, however proud,
> Contained in their afflatus the reproach
> That first drove Crispin to his wandering.
> He could not be content with counterfeit,
> With masquerade of thought, with shapeless words
> That must belie the racking masquerade,
> With fictive flourishes that preordained
> His passion's permit, hang of coat, degree
> Of buttons, measure of his salt. Such trash
> Might help the blind, not him, serenely sly.
> It irked his patience.[23]

One wonders whether any obsession can more unsettle the writer of poetry than the indispensable obsession with truth, whether any curiosity can make his task of creation more difficult than curiosity about the ultimate nature of reality. Were Stevens the aesthetic fop that so many contemporaneous readers of *Harmonium* believed him to be, he would have found no grounds for distrusting the romantic incantations of "Sunday Morning"—although it is probable that he would have found no inspiration to write it. His difficulty was that the only poetry he could find ultimately satisfying was poetry of a kind that neither his own skepticism nor the hard contours of the modern world would countenance. For all its impassioned dignity, "Sunday Morning" is, in its primitivism, "Related in romance to backward flights"; for all the beauty of its evocation, it is, as poetry must be, as tenuous in its sanctions as those birdsongs of which the lady says:

> . . . *"I am content when wakened birds*
> *Before they fly, test the reality*
> *Of misty fields, by their sweet questionings;*
> *But when the birds are gone, and their warm fields*
> *Return no more, where, then, is paradise?"*

And for all the artistry of its rhetoric, it is "counterfeit";[24] it offers a verbal and philosophical masquerade that may have been workaday costume in the past and could conceivably become so again in the future, but which cannot but distort the present reality, and cannot help but preordain, for him who chooses to wear it, "passion's permit, hang of coat, degree/ Of buttons, measure of his salt"—for to adopt the style of a former tradition is perforce to adopt its vision. Excursions such as "Sunday Morning" must come to seem bland to those inclined to mistrust the comforts of an outworn romantic tradition. The grand style revived was not, for Stevens, what the modern poem had to be: "The poem of the mind in the act of finding/ What will suffice"; it is rather the reiteration of a satisfaction already found, a repetition of "what/ Was already in the script."

V

Thirteen Ways

As POET AND AS A MAN of his time, Stevens could take but cold comfort in the temporal realities of the twentieth century. Yet, more intensely than the most avuncular of his critics, Stevens understood from the start that his conception of art as a means of recovering pleasure was threatened and could be destroyed by an aestheticism whose satisfactions were drawn solely from the imagination's desires. If poetry is in fact to provide the reason for and mode of being which, in ages of belief, were provided by religion,[1] it is essential that imaginative experience have its foundation in reality. If it does not, its achievements, like those of the dead romantic, will "lie in minor wish-fulfillments and [be] incapable of abstraction."[2] Once more, then, we see why the relationship between the imagination and reality raised for Stevens so exigent a problem. Only through the exploration of this relationship would it be possible to demonstrate that poetry's vaunting claims were founded on ground more substantial than faith.

To hold himself responsible to the claims of reality, however, was not for a poet of Stevens' temperament an easy obligation. Stevens was far from certain that contemporary reality—so unprecedentedly responsive to the claims of reason and indifferent to the needs of the spirit—might not prove intractable to the imagination's shaping. It should be clear that a poet afflicted with such doubts may yield to them without ceasing to be a poet. If we indeed live in a world that has become totally alien to the world of poetry, those anachronistic figures who, despite the insistence of reason, still find it necessary to create, are left with two alternatives. They may, as Eliot for example has done, create a poetry—essentially a poetry of lamentation—whose major theme is precisely that contemporary reality is no longer adequate to the demands of art. Such a poetry, however, inasmuch as it is a repudiation of life, must also at its core be a repudiation of art; from Stevens' viewpoint, at least, art springs from love of the world, a world which, paradoxically, art teaches us how to love. It is to the art that is really anti-art that Stevens alludes when he remarks: "Most modern reproducers of life, even including the camera, really repudiate it. We gulp down evil, choke at good."[3] Stevens himself, of course, wrote poems on the impossibility of writing poems, in which he acknowledged that contemporary reality, northern reality, was too frigid an environment for art. Yet although he could at times present the poet as "The Man Whose Pharynx Was Bad"—could at times yield his art to themes of renunciation and aesthetic defeat—his life as an artist depended on his refusal ultimately to succumb to "the malady of the quotidian";[4] his creative winters were sunless and death-dealing, but they were interludes, never the final climate of his mind.

The second possible response to one's sense of a world hostile to the aggrandizement of art is to insist that the values which nurture the spirit, the melodies which please the ear, are the possessions of the past;

and that we can come no closer to recovering them than by evoking their echoes from the past, their proper domain. The use to which contemporary poets have put primitive myth and dead literary traditions is at root this negative use of contrasting the sordid and shapeless present with some radiant and coherent past. The second mode of response, like the first, had strong attractions for Stevens; and one could easily imagine him, had his generation been earlier and his imagination less intrepid, at home with his pre-Raphaelite forebears, who came to easy terms with the painful facts of their world by retiring to the Palace of Art and the pleasures of dim time. As matters actually stood, however, despite the ardor with which he longed for the comforts of a real or imagined past, Stevens was incapable of retiring to worlds that did not exist. Art founded on such retirement, Stevens insisted, can today no more nourish us than the poetry of Sir Walter Scott, which, in Stevens' words, "is like the scenery of a play that has come to an end. It is scenery that has been trucked away and stored somewhere on the horizon or just below. In short, the world of Sir Walter Scott no longer exists."[5]

Operating singly, the two modes of poetic response threaten the death of art. The first, by mirroring a stupefying chaos that it can no longer order, becomes part of the shapelessness it reflects. The second, by confining itself to nostalgia for scenery that no longer has models outside the mind, reduces poetry to the opiate the "realist" believes it to be. Thus, the dilemma the contemporary artist has shared with most of his fellows is that, while convinced of the spiritual poverty of the present, he can find little ground for faith in richer times to come. His dreams are of unregainable golden ages of the past rather than of achievable utopias of the future. Art that *does* insist on the necessity of our emancipation from the past in order to achieve a more satisfying future—art, that is, like William Blake's or D. H. Lawrence's—our age is inclined to dismiss as "sentimental" or "mystical," as if the only realism we can still conceive is the realism of despair.

Insofar as the present age has given itself to such realism, it has given itself to death, since, in a fallen world at least,[6] the pulse of life is beat out by the diastole of "ought to be" against the systole of "is." The pressures of our own time have tended to break this rhythm, to segment the process into its parts. Witnesses to and in one way or another participants in the breakdown of religious belief and the continual collapse of what had once seemed eternal verities, resigned to the belief that to maintain the vision of what ought to be is a form of sentimental weakness, most serious contemporary artists have assumed the task of portraying, as honestly as possible, as ruthlessly as necessary, the "is" upon which the facts of our particular time insist. Undeniably this task *is* a necessary one; only through its performance can art strip away the dead fictions which periodically stultify both art and life. But the stage of purgation is only a stage. Unless—and this too is possible—we are at the end of history, it continues to be the mind's delight and burden to create new fictions, new structures of belief and hope that can bear up under the pressures of contemporary experience as the old structures can no longer.[7]

The impetus of Stevens' art is to preserve the life-rhythm that flows from the tension between reality and desire, and the evolution of his art stems from the necessity of continuously restoring the balance between the contraries without which there is no progression. This balance is by nature impermanent, since new events in the life of the individual and of the race constitute new pressures of reality to which the imagination must respond if it is to remain alive. Conversely, each new claim of the imagination will evoke a response from the creator's own "reality-principle"; these claims will be relinquished or maintained depending on whether or not they successfully withstand the test imposed on them by reality. This conception of the poetic (or imaginative) activity as a continuous process of dialectical testing and revision is implicit in Stevens' definition of the modern poem as "The poem of the mind in the act of finding/ What will suffice," as it is implicit in the poem in which the definition appears.[8]

In sum, the dialectical pattern of the poetic process that emerges from Stevens' practice and theory is this. The imagination, reacting against the inadequacies and negative pressures of reality, strives to create for itself a pleasure palace, a heterocosm in which the desires of the mind and sense can fully be gratified. Achievement of this goal, however, is equivalent to total detachment from things as they are. Art produced in this manner can make no claims to any truth but the truth of our desire; and thus, from Stevens' viewpoint, such art is identical with religion, as a projection of need, hallucinatory in the same sense that a starving man's vision of food or an isolated man's vision of women is hallucinatory. If poetry is to be more than hallucination, it is necessary that the imagination be checked by reality. To create such poetry is an onerous task, since reality, if not literally chaotic, resists all human attempts to reduce it to tidy forms; thus the poem that attempts to mirror reality must either be a reflection of chaos or, if it imposes a form on reality, must be a simplification and therefore a distortion of its subject. Fluctuating, then, between the imagination's desire for the harmonious forms it envisages, and the reason's insistence that the poem must be a reflection of truth, the poetic process is a process of interminable conflict.

This being for Stevens the case, how are we to explain the fact that he continued to write poems, only to record anew the inability of art to bring these conflicting drives to any final reconciliation? Or, to put the problem differently, how are we to account for the fact that in two poems, both published in 1940, Stevens could insist, first, that "It can never be satisfied, the mind, never," and second, "That the mind is the end and must be satisfied"?[9] To answer this question is also to explain Stevens' particular utopian vision. Stevens has offended politically liberal critics by his refusal to deal with social evils in social terms; yet it is possible that by his very insistence on dealing with them in aesthetic terms, he cut more deeply toward the core of such evils than would otherwise have been possible. To put the matter as succinctly as possible, there can be no end to the frustration of the artist and to the dialectic that springs from that frustration until the world of the imagination's desire becomes identical with the world of reality. As society now stands, such a possibility must in itself be a pipedream. It could be a genuine possibility only if all men were poets, that is, men of imagination. When Stevens speaks of the hero, the superman, he does not refer to the man of power in the ordinary sense, but rather to the man of imaginative power, the man capable of *desiring* (and therefore, conceivably, of creating) a world that could satisfy the imagination's highest visions. Only for such a man and through such a man can the world's darkness be lifted; men without the hope that springs from vision are condemned to dwell in a world that reflects their despair, and serve, willy nilly, to perpetuate that black world without imagination. For Stevens, then, aesthetic and socio-political questions are inextricably fused: "Politic man has ordained/ Imagination as the fateful sin."[10] Even in a world without imagination, however, renascence remains possible as long as some among us retain the capacity to perceive that "The sun is seeking something bright to shine on,"[11] to believe that

> *The night should be warm and fluter's fortune*
> *Should play in the trees when morning comes.*
>
> *Once it was, the repose of night,*
> *Was a place, strong place, in which to sleep.*
> *It is shaken now. It will burst into flames,*
> *Either now or tomorrow or the day after that.*[12]

Stevens' poetry, my preceding remarks have been designed to suggest, records the struggles of a contemporary mind to preserve its own and its society's capacity for utopian vision. The record is as frequently marked by anguish and futility as by tentative success because, although more basically for aesthetic than for political reasons, Stevens shared the skepticism toward utopian vision characteristic of his age. Paradise cannot be regained, he believed, if we succumb to an all-embracing and all-destroying rationalism that closes the doors to vision. Neither, however, can it be regained if the potential redeemer, the man of imagination, allows *himself* to succumb to an art whose achievement "lies in minor wish-fulfillments," in defeatist escapism. Thus, before we can examine in detail the ultimate claims Stevens was prepared to make for poetry as a means of bringing about man's rebirth, it will be useful first to study the dialectical process itself, the process by which Stevens raised for himself, if he did not answer, all the destructive arguments that reason may bring to bear against the imagination's boasts.

Not surprisingly, the poetic structure in which Stevens cast these arguments with himself is frequently dramatic. This is particularly true in *Harmonium,* where we find a number of poems that present a latent or manifest conflict between a figure representing the poet and another (or others) representing a force that threatens or mocks his ambitions. Frequently, as in the group of poems I shall first discuss, the poet-figure himself remains the mute and passive subject of the abuse or advise of the speaker. Thus, in "The Plot Against the Giant"[13] the poet, although a giant, is from the viewpoint of the girls who plot his overthrow a maundering yokel, the appropriately foolish giant of fairy tale. The girls themselves are in effect his senses of smell, sight, and hearing. The first girl proposes to check him with "the civilest odors/ . . . Of geraniums and unsmelled flowers," the second to abash him with "Arching cloths besprinkled with colors/ As small as fish-eggs," and the third to undo him by whispering in his ear "Heavenly labials in a world of gutturals." Their plot, in short, is to offer him the sensual gratifications to which he is most susceptible. Although the charm of this poem is in its totally unexpected viewpoint, we observe that even in this relatively unambitious exercise, Stevens broaches a highly serious theme. The poet, a giant prepared to engage in large exploits (whetting his hacker"), is in danger of being unmanned by the feminine susceptibility to sensual appeal that is part of what makes him a poet. Stevens' preoccupation here, as, more ambitiously, in "The Ordinary Women" published five years later, is with the Palace of Art theme; and he did not require the subsequent warnings of his critics to convince him that the appeal of sensual-aestheticism was one of the forces that could unman his art. The verb "unman" has special appropriateness here, since in

"The Plot Against the Giant" we have one of the earliest examples of Stevens' identification of the female with sensual appeal in the broadest sense. Stevens consistently conceives of the reality-principle as male, of the pleasure-principle as female. This symbolic pattern helps explain why, in "Sunday Morning," it is a woman (or, more precisely, the female side of Stevens' own mind) who in contentment still feels "the need of some imperishable bliss."[14] The pattern is made explicit in the late poem "Farewell without a Guitar," where Stevens speaks "of male reality/ And of that other and her desire."[15]

In "Bantams in Pine-Woods,"[16] published in 1922, Stevens employed a dramatic form and *persona* for the poet similar to those he had used in "The Plot Against the Giant," only this time the dialectical conflict is between the poet's desire for universal forms and reality's insistence on the truth and significance of particulars. Iffucan, who shares with Stevens a "portly" frame, an appetite for universals, and, as his name suggests, a faith in grand possibilities, is for all his vaunting "hoos" a metaphysical strutter who would reduce reality to the services of his own falsifying imagination. His progress is appropriately arrested by the inchling, who speaks for the personal, concrete reality the giant has ignored. It would be a mistake, however, to assume that because the inchling does all the talking, we are to identify his position with Stevens' own. As usual, Stevens is maintaining two arguments in delicate ironic balance. Both Iffucan *and* the inchling are bantams: Iffucan because, for all his swagger, the potency of his imagination depends on self-delusion, falsification of reality; and the inchling because, although he is more in harmony with his soil than Iffucan, the particulars of experience for which he speaks exist in themselves and for themselves, and thus deny the possibility of art, of structured imaginative response.

113

It is possible to suggest once more through "Bantams" how, for readers familiar with "the whole of Harmonium," each of Stevens' lyrics suggests the lineaments of his total field of concerns. Thus, just as in the second two lines of the poem the inchling mocks Iffucan's delusions of metaphysical grandeur, so in the first two he ridicules Iffucan's bombastic rhetoric in much the same way that Stevens ridiculed his own in "The Comedian as the Letter C." Still another example of the way in which Stevens' dominant preoccupations appear in least likely places is the association of Iffucan, through his title and costume, with the tropics, and of the inchling, through his reference to the pines and "their Appalachian tangs," with the north. Through these oblique geographical symbols, the slight lyric blossoms into a microcosmic representation of Stevens' aesthetic cosmos. Iffucan becomes, among other things, a southern (romantic) intruder on the inchling's northern (realistic) domain; the luxuriant costume in which the southern poet went garbed is ridiculous when seen against the bristling realities of the north. Through these terms, "Bantams in Pine-Woods" may be seen as an anticipation of "Farewell to Florida."

The function of dramatic form in the two lyrics I have been discussing is to allow Stevens objective expression of conflicting aspects of his own mind. When he speaks of himself, in "Thirteen Ways of Looking at a Blackbird," as being "of three minds,/ Like a tree/ In which there are three blackbirds,"[17] Stevens provides us with a skeleton key to his thought. His mind habitually operates like a conversation between friends—or enemies—seeking to reconcile diverse or conflicting points of view. What makes for difficulty in interpreting poems of this kind is not the abstruseness but rather the subjectivity of their thought. Such poems are not *about* their apparent subjects, but rather employ those subjects to project their true concern: the imitation of the mind that makes them. In Stevens' words, they are poems "of the act of the mind."[18]

Coming late in the *Harmonium* period, "Bantams in Pine-Woods" is a commentary on the lavish, imaginatively indulgent poetry that dominates Stevens' first book, a poetry which, this early, at least part of his mind was turning against. That the dissatisfaction with the *Harmonium* group he was later to record in his letter to Harriet Monroe[19] was indeed genuine, and in part responsible for his temporary abandonment of poetry, is suggested once more by the poem of latest composition to be collected in the first edition of *Harmonium*. "Floral Decorations for Bananas,"[20] first published in April 1923 as part of a group entitled "New England Pieces," is another dramatic monologue directed against a poet of luxurious tastes who seeks through art the unhampered gratification of his desire for sensual pleasure and the free indulgence of his imagination. This time, however, the poet appears not in the guise of a fatuous giant or exotic chieftain but rather in that of inept table decorator.

The parallels between "Floral Decorations for Bananas" and "Bantams in Pine-Woods" are of more than incidental interest, since one of Stevens' most remarkable qualities is his ability to express similar themes in poems of radically different surfaces. It is because of this quality that Stevens is able to indulge his appetite for "mere repititions," as he calls them in "Notes Toward a Supreme Fiction."[21] The motive for such repetition is not paucity of experience, but rather the desire to repeat pleasurable experience. "Children," Freud observed, "cannot have their *pleasurable* experiences repeated often enough," in contrast to the adult, for whom "novelty is always the condition of enjoyment."[22] As a diligent scholar of pleasure, Stevens recognized this pattern that relates the poet to the child. Thus, in the passage from "Notes Toward a Supreme Fiction" cited above:

> Red robin, stop in your preludes, practicing
> Mere repetitions. These things at least comprise
> An occupation, an exercise, a work,
>
> A thing final in itself, and, therefore, good:
> One of the vast repetitions final in
> Themselves and, therefore, good, the going round
>
> And round and round, the merely going round,
> Until merely going round is a final good,
> The way wine comes at a table in a wood.

To observe this "merely going round" in practice: Iffucan's extravagant title and dress in "Bantams" become the "insolent linear peels/ And sullen hurricane shapes" of bananas in "Floral Decorations," while the Appalachian pines of the first poem become the civil, nontropical eglantine of the second. As Iffucan was a fish painfully out of water among the inchling's pines, so the tropical bananas clash with the eglantine. Finally, as the lofty metaphysical ambitions of the poet are mocked in "Bantams" by the inchling's abuse and the comic grandiloquence of Iffucan's title, so, in "Floral Decorations" the speaker's addressing the inept decorator as "nuncle" mocks Stevens' own fondness for the archaisms by which, half-ironically, he evokes a more radiant past. We are thus plunged once more into the conflict of north and south, and once more made to see how acutely Stevens sensed the inappropriateness of his luxuriant, imaginatively indulgent art to the time and place in which he happened to live.

Where "Floral Decorations" goes further than "Bantams" is in its final insistence not on one style of "decoration" or another, but on a harmony between style and environment.[23] Either, the speaker insists, replace the bananas with plums in an "eighteenth century dish," thus providing a harmonious setting "For the women of primrose and purl,/ Each one in her decent curl"; or, if civility is not the aim of the decor, let the setting be adjusted to the bananas, and the guests in turn will be transformed from decent figures in lace to alluringly indecent women, "all shanks/ And bangles and slatted eyes." That this latter, radically un-New England decor ultimately has the greater appeal to the speaker (and, we assume, to the poet) is suggested in the last stanza, where the bananas are in effect defined as concrete images of the sensual, even sexual, and, by New England standards, "indecent" imagination. If we are to decorate with bananas, adjures the speaker,

> . . . *deck the bananas in leaves*
> *Plucked from the Carib trees,*
> *Fibrous and dangling down,*
> *Oozing cantankerous gum*
> *Out of their purple maws,*
> *Darting out of their purple craws*
> *Their musky and tingling tongues.*[24]

It seems hardly extravagant to suggest at this point that Stevens shared with Freud the conviction that temporal happiness is attainable only through a release from sensual and sexual repression.

One key to Stevens' method in the last two poems I have discussed is his statement in the essay "Imagination as Value" that "Costume is an instance of imaginative life as social form."[25] The banana decor, no less than Iffucan's robes and title, is an instance of romantic cos-

tume—romantic in the sense that Stevens borrows
approvingly from Irving Babbitt: "A thing is romantic
when it is strange, unexpected, intense, superlative,
extreme, unique, etc." To these categories, however,
Stevens adds another: "It must also be living. It must
always be living. It is in the sense of living intensity,
living singularity that it is the vital element in poetry."[26]
"Floral Decorations" thus helps us to understand why
Stevens indulged in imaginative extravagance and put
on bizarre masks even in poems in which he was mock-
ing these very characteristics in himself. If Iffucan
and bananas are absurdly out of harmony with their
environment, if, as Stevens put it in 1935, the poet in
our time is "A most inappropriate man/ In a most inaus-
picious place,"[27] the necessary task of restoring harmony
must come not merely from the poet's efforts to adjust
to his environment but also from the environment's
efforts to adjust to the poet. If it is necessary to sacrifice
"the sense of living intensity, living singularity," to a
world that has no stomach for these qualities, then it is
necessary to sacrifice poetry altogether.

To maintain these qualities in a world that finds no
place for them can, however, be a heavy task, as Stevens
makes clear in "The Weeping Burgher."[28] One is op-
pressed by "the sorry verities," by one's awareness that
the beauty created is the projection of desire for what
should but does not exist.

> The sorry verities!
> Yet in excess, continual,
> There is cure of sorrow.

We thus see the other side of the coin we have been
examining. True, the imagination must be held in check
by reality; but so, if life is to be supportable, reality must
be enriched by the imagination. This, essentially, is the

theme of "The Revolutionists Stop for Orangeade,"[29] which first appeared in the second edition of *Harmonium* and which is probably the wittiest of Stevens' several commentaries on his own "essential gawdiness."

"The Revolutionists Stop for Orangeade," like the other dramatic monologues I have been examining, remains a difficult poem only until we have established the symbolic identities of its actors; its meaning becomes clear enough once we recognize that the revolutionary captain ("Capitán profundo, capitán geloso") is the poet and that the speakers are, most probably, his own unwritten poems, although they may also be understood as the same audience which in "The Man with the Blue Guitar," demands of the poet "A tune beyond us as we are/ Yet nothing changed by the blue guitar."[30] The orangeade the revolutionists stop for is equivalent to "A tune beyond us as we are": Stevens frequently employs food and drink, ranging from possum, sop, and taters[31] to the wine of Montrachet-le-Jardin,[32] to represent the good, the pleasure, we desire; and in bad times only the imagination can satisfy that desire.

"Ask us not to sing standing in the sun," the chorus insists, as if in reply to the poet who was more and more strenuously to demand of his poems that they "adhere to reality."[33]

> *Ask us not to sing standing in the sun,*
> *Hairy-backed and hump-armed,*
> *Flat-ribbed and big-bagged.*
> *There is no pith in music*
> *Except in something false.*

The particular false music they request is in the form of "a song of serpent-kin,/ Necks among the thousand leaves,/ Tongues among the fruit"; and the allusion to "serpent-kin"[34] is not, as might first appear, a reference to the biblical fall but rather carries us back to that "something serpentine" which the speaker of "Floral Decorations" insists that the bananas require, and with which indeed, the bananas are provided in the baroquely serpentine last stanza of their poem.

But "The Revolutionists Stop for Orangeade" is concerned not only with the fecund invention which poetry must provide to make less sorry the "Hairy-backed and hump-armed" human condition. It also suggests that the poet must wear a costume as eccentric and bizarre as the songs he sings, must, in the end, play the role of the clown who laughs in order not to weep, who embellishes that which, unembellished, is not to be borne; he will wear not the square hat of the rationalist[35] but, rather, " a helmet without reason./ Tufted, tilted, twirled, and twisted." He will, in short, be Iffucan once more, but shrunk from ten-foot stature, his chieftain's robes changed for those of the wise fool, who knowingly creates for himself and for us the intense and singular illusions without which we cannot live:

> *Hang a feather by your eye,*
> *Nod and look a little sly.*
> *This must be the vent of pity,*
> *Deeper than a truer ditty*
> *Of the real that wrenches,*
> *Of the quick that's wry.*

It will be clear now that for Stevens the conflict between north and south, reality and the imagination, the reality-principle and the pleasure-principle, may also be understood as a conflict between theories of art. The poetic speculations on the relationship between reality and the imagination that I have been examining seem an attempt to escape from the rigid demands of a purely mimetic theory of art, and at the same time to justify the poet against the charge that insofar as he enriches reality, he lies. To accomplish these purposes without violating his own axiom that "There is nothing so oppressive to a man of intellectual principle as unprincipled thinking,"[36] it was necessary for Stevens to adhere to a concept of reality that includes "a world of poetry indistinguishable from the world in which we live, or, I ought to say, . . . from the world in which we shall come to live, since what makes the poet the potent figure he is, or was, or ought to be, is that he creates the world to which we turn incessantly and without knowing it and that he gives to life the supreme fictions without which we are unable to conceive it."[37] However alien it may be to contemporary taste, this conception of poetic reality has an ancient pedigree. Indeed, Stevens' remark closely echoes, presumably without intending to, that of the neo-classical French critic, Charles Batteux, who, in his *Les Beaux Arts réduit à un même principe* (1747) wrote of the heightened nature—*la belle nature*—of art that it is not "le vrai qui est; mais le vrai qui peut être, le beau vrai, qui est représenté comme s'il existoit réellement, & avec toutes les perfections qu'il peut recevoir."[38]

Stevens wrote in an age whose poetry and poetics tended to be increasingly skeptical about the artist's obligation or capacity to represent *la belle nature,* and which in its central trends, has abandoned the figure of the lamp to return to the earlier figure of the mirror as apt symbol of the artist's relationship to reality. Yet Stevens' instinctive poetic loyalties were to a romantic conception of art; his object, no less than that of his romantic forebears, was, in the words M. H. Abrams uses to describe the aim of early nineteenth-century aesthetic theorists, "To overcome the sense of man's alienation from the world by healing the cleavage between subject and object, between the vital, purposeful, value-full world of private experience and the dead postulated world of extension, quantity, and motion."[39]

Expressive art in this sense is confronted by a dilemma. Although, in its intitial intention, such art withdraws from the external world, the "objective" world, in an attempt to recover sources by which the cleavage between subject and object might be healed, the historical evolution of expressive theory and practice during the nineteenth century, culminating in the doctrines of the art for art's sake movement, widens the cleavage which the expressive theories were originally designed to close. The art of the *fin de siècle* is in at least one sense an expression of aesthetic defeatism, in that it surrenders all questions of public reality to the increasingly rationalistic modes of inquiry, and makes no claims for art beyond its own internal integrity.

That Stevens cannot properly be classed with those for whom the poetic experience was purely private and subjective experience I have already tried to suggest. What his early admirers mistook to be preciosity and dandyism was in fact an attempt to forge a world of art capable of withstanding the most vitriolic tests of reality. Thus tested, that world could responsibly be offered as a model for a new reality, one in which "vital, purposeful, value-full" experience could be possible in public as well as private modes. One of the failures of Romantic poetry, after all, was that it allowed its Iffucans to roam unchecked by inchlings, and set its tables with bananas without regarding the incongruity between the fruit and the world in which it would be eaten. In Stevens' words, "What happened, as we were traversing the whole heaven, is that the imagination lost its power to sustain us. It has the strength of reality or none at all."[40] Stevens was unwilling to repeat the error, and as a man equally at home in the public and private worlds, he was particularly responsive to and better prepared to grapple with the objections of "realists" that poetry has nothing to do with reality. Without the most acute awareness of "le vrai qui est," Stevens' work insists, there is little possibility of projecting a meaningful vision of "le vrai qui peut etre." The task is thus to produce an art that is equally responsive to the demands of mimetic and expressive theory.

Throughout *Harmonium,* as we have seen, there is reflected a conflict between a poetry that has the strength of reality and a poetry that embellishes a reality which, naked, is not to be borne. Implicit in each of these conceptions is a nagging question. First, assuming that the task of the poet *is* to mirror reality, is it *possible* for the poem, whatever its intentions, to hold up a nondistorting mirror to the world. Second, assuming, as Stevens puts it in "Sketch of the Ultimate Politician," that the task of the poet is to be "the final builder of the total building,/ The final dreamer of the total dream,"[41] will not the achievement of absolute harmony, total metaphor—in short, of the ultimate reality Stevens constantly pursues—contain in itself the destruction of poetry? Poetry, after all, is the manipulation of particulars in pursuit of universals. However, as Northrop Frye has pointed out, an art that can be structured around an intellectual absolute may be compared "to a night in which all cows are black, a world clearly no improvement on 'reality,' which is also one color."[42] The second problem, then, can be put this way. Poetry reacts against chaos by pursuing patterns of universal order, indulging the mind's desire for resemblance.[43] Fully to satisfy that desire, however, fully to envisage a world in which "A man and a woman and a blackbird/ Are one,"[44] is to move into a stasis closely akin to death. A world of perfectly harmonious form may be metaphysically satisfying, but it is not a world in which the mind can any longer "act," and thus not a world that can engender poetry.

It should be apparent that these two questions stemming from the possibility of a truly mimetic art are not aesthetic questions in any narrow sense. They have immensely to do with the urgent contemporary *social* problem of the artist in isolation.[45] If contemporary reality is the moral and ideological chaos most modern artists have argued it to be, will it be necessary for the artist of the future, still seeking to satisfy his hunger for order, to withdraw more and more deeply into a contemplation of his art as its own subject, and to forego finally and without qualification any vision of himself as a man speaking to men, teaching them to see their world more vividly and therefore more lovingly than they would be able to do without him? That possibility is implicit in a conception of art which can no longer hold the imagination and reality in equal balance, and Stevens repeatedly confronted the possibility, although he was unwilling to accept it as a necessary final condition. With Camus, he perceived that "The most striking feature of the world we live in is that most of its inhabitants —with the exception of pietests of various kinds—are cut off from the future. Life has no validity unless it can project itself toward the future, can ripen and progress."[46] If literature itself, the instrument by which men have always been supplied with visions of a future, abnegates that function, the domination of fatalism and death would appear complete.

To a frightening degree contemporary men of letters appear to accept that domination as a *fait accompli,* and give evidence that the cold war has thoroughly paralyzed the private as well as the public sensibility.

Thus William Phillips, in his introduction to a book by Frank Kermode, can without apparent irony praise Kermode's "feeling for the contemporary (which usually means the ability to cope with things that are not grandiose or permanent)."[47] Then, expanding his analysis of contemporary life and letters, Phillips observes:

> Though we cannot conceal our nostalgia for the twenties and thirties, we try to keep any tendency toward literary or political radicalism from getting out of hand. Hence we play up the virtues of "maturity" and "responsibility." Criticism, which is usually the first to make its peace with its time, has dutifully responded by putting a high premium on intelligence and catholicity. Thus it frowns on movements, crusades, doctrines, on any extreme stand that might jar the prevailing equilibrium.[48]

That Phillips' account of the current function of criticism—and, by extension, of literature generally—is as valid as it is depressing may in part stem from the failure of modern letters to take up the questions with which Stevens' poetry grapples. To explore, as Stevens insisted on doing, the uses of imaginative experience in the modern world is nothing short of exploring the possibility of a sequel to the modern world.

The second of the questions I raised a moment ago will be met directly in my concluding chapter, and cannot be approached until we have grappled with the first: is a truly mimetic art possible? The answer that Stevens' art provides is a qualified no. Although art grows out of reality, or what Aristotle called nature, it is not and cannot be imitation of reality.[49] As we discover in such poems as "Earthy Anecdote," "Valley Candle," "Anecdote of the Jar," and "Thirteen Ways of Looking at a Blackbird," the imagination, in its hunger for order, imposes its patterns on the external world, and it is through these patterns that we may achieve, momentarily, understanding of and tenuous harmony with that world. But the patterns are ours, not the world's. Always eluding the nets of order that the imagination throws out is "the irreducible X,"[50] the essential reality which, like the sea, is inhuman, protean.

Yet, if the earth is not our own, neither are we truly aliens from it. It takes from us the only meanings it can know, as when, in "The Idea of Order at Key West," in response to the solitary girl's song, "the sea/ Whatever self it had, became the self/ That was her song."[51] And we take from it the matter of our song, which springs both from our desire to be at one with things as they are and from our awareness that one of the prices of our humanity is our inability to achieve that oneness:[52]

From this the poem springs: that we live in a place
That is not our own and, much more, not ourselves.[53]

Let me turn, then, to a group of early poems in which we may see this process of alternating harmony and alienation at work. In "Earthy Anecdote,"[54] the first poem of Stevens' first volume, a reality that is shapelessness and flux is symbolized by a herd of bucks clattering over Oklahoma (in the language of Stevens' geographical symbolism the arid southwest is generally an emblem of chaos, of a primitive and unformed nature). The firecat, on the other hand—a beast that does not exist in nature—plays the role of the imagination. As it forces the galloping bucks to swerve, "in a swift, circular line," first to the right and then to the left, it momentarily gives order to flux, imposing forms where they did not exist. But the order imposed by the imagination is essentially arbitrary: the bucks can be moved to right and to left, but they continue clattering. And imaginative order, the poem concludes, is ephemeral as well as arbitrary:

> *Later, the firecat closed his bright eyes*
> *And slept.*

We must follow the symbols beyond the poem and see the bucks resume their wild course with no firecat to check and direct them. A poem, like this poem, resembles a camera: it orders reality by freezing its image. But the bucks continue running even after the shutter clicks closed, even after the negative is developed and printed and pasted into the family album. As Northrop Frye puts it, "The 'act of the mind' in which the imagination begins . . . is an arresting of a flow of perceptions without and of impressions within. In that arrest there is born the principle of form or order: the inner violence of the imagination is a 'rage for order.' "[55]

"Earthy Anecdote" offers a rebuttal to those who complain that poetry lies, to those who say: "You have a blue guitar,/ You do not play things as they are."[56] The very processes of knowing and perceiving are lies, the poem argues, and poetry is superior to other forms of epistemological lying in that it is capable of perceiving more acutely its true relationship with things as they are.

In "Valley Candle"[57] Stevens confronts the same problem with the same ironic awareness; only the symbol is changed. The artificial light of the candle for a moment gives shape to the "beams of the huge night" that converge upon it, as the firecat imposed pattern on the clattering bucks. The candle gives light, but flickering light, threatened by the wind and dwarfed by the darkness of the immense valley for which it can momentarily provide a center, a focal point, a mode of composition. In the end, however, as "the firecat closed his bright eyes/

And slept," so here, when the wind blows the candle will go out. Yet, although the initial act of the imagination must eventually succumb to the chaos it opposes, the act, when it takes the form of a poem, enjoys the same permanence that in "Sunday Morning" Stevens attributes to "April's green":[58] the permanence of recurrence. Reader finds himself allied with poet in the permanent guerilla warfare against chaos; thus, each reading of the poem—ideally, of any poem—is a rekindling of the candle. This, I believe, is the logic behind the poem's structure: in the first three lines the beams of night converge upon the candle itself, "Until the wind blew"; in the last three, the beams converge upon the candle's image —in effect upon the poem itself. The extinguishing of the flame marks the final end of the initial imaginative act; the extinguishing of the image marks the end of that act as it has been reexperienced by the reader.

The two poems I have discussed, and "Anecdote of the Jar" to which I will turn next, are like monads, not only because they constitute the primitive elements of Stevens' poetic universe, but also because, like monads, they reflect that total universe from their own special point of view. As primitives, they are unlike some of Stevens' later, more discursive, poems in that they use the method of epiphany: they allow "general truths" to *show forth* through concrete images, but do not attempt to talk *about* these truths. Like Chesterton's dogmas, they are "like a flash of lightning—an instantaneous lucidity that opens across a whole landscape."

In discussing Stevens' poetic explorations of mimesis, I have so far emphasized, first, that insofar as the imagination checks the flow of perceptions in the process of ordering them into impressions, it necessarily distorts things as they are; and second, that this act of checking is arbitrary (the particular poem is one of many possible versions of the reality it represents) and temporary (even when given the permanence of poetic form, it requires the reader's imaginative response before it can be repeated, and each repetition of the imaginative act, each total response to the poem, is in itself a temporary and isolated experience). A further limitation to the imagination's efforts to mirror reality is suggested by "Anecdote of the Jar."[59] Here, more explicitly than in "Earthy Anecdote" or "Valley Candle," the imaginative act (or poem—there is no essential difference) in the form of a man-made object, orders and tames the wilderness around it by providing a form around which that wilderness can compose itself.[60] "Anecdote of the Jar," however, takes a more negative view of the imagination than do the other two poems; whereas the firecat has a vitality of its own, and the candle at least throws off light, the jar is colorless and sterile:

> *It took dominion everywhere.*
> *The jar was gray and bare.*
> *It did not give of bird or bush,*
> *Like nothing else in Tennessee.*

The imagination may create versions of the world, and, as Roy Harvey Pearce suggests, the versions it creates "come to be versions of itself in the act of exercising its primary function: at least, to realize its humanity; at the most, to make men more human."[61] Granting that fact, however, we must not mistake the version for the thing itself: the well-spring of life's vitality and color is that same "slovenly wilderness" the imagination is at such pains to tidy. I do not believe it is claiming too much for "Valley Candle" to suggest that in it we find a rejection of any theory of art that assumes the imagination can function independently of reality. Stevens would have had little sympathy with the painter Bernard Buffet, whose house in the Basses Alpes "is specially designed to exclude the beautiful views that other people would dote upon. Nothing must disturb his imagination."[62]

It would be a mistake to assume that because Stevens recognized the limitations of the imagination he suffered the recognition gladly. Throughout these poems and throughout his work he records his impatience with the conviction his experience forced upon him: that there is no *one* order which firecat or candle or jar can strive to impose. The form they provide is nearly as arbitrary and shifting as the "reality" they are designed to control. This is the shaping idea behind the famous "Thirteen Ways of Looking at a Blackbird,"[63] a poem in which we perceive more clearly the role of metaphor in the poetic exploration of truth.

The poem operates as a series of variations on a theme. Its opening stanza deliberately isolates the merest minuscule of reality:

> *Among twenty mountains*
> *The only moving thing*
> *Was the eye of a blackbird.*

The subsequent twelve stanzas represent the mind's effort to find meaning in that simplest fact. But meaning cannot reside in the thing in itself; if it did, the first stanza would be a completed poem. The mind seeks meaning through discovery of resemblance, through metaphor; and each subsequent stanza offers a metaphoric context against which the moving eye can find meaning. To argue, as does Roy Harvey Pearce, that the thirteen ways of looking at a blackbird "are perhaps dominated by this one":

> *A man and a woman*
> *Are one.*

130

Thirteen Ways

> *A man and a woman and a blackbird*
> *Are one,*

is altogether to distort the point of the poem. Stevens is not saying, as Pearce would have us believe, that "The truth about the imagination is that it can again and again bring about such unity in the world."[64] He is saying rather that, *although* the imagination can repeatedly bring about such unity, each of its unifying achievements represents one of an infinity of possible unities, and more, each unity requires a distortion of the perceived object itself. Thus to say that

> *I was of three minds,*
> *Like a tree*
> *In which there are three blackbirds,*

is no longer to speak about the moving eye, or even about the bird, but rather about the mind. To say,

> *I do not know which to prefer,*
> *The beauty of inflections*
> *Or the beauty of innuendoes,*
> *The blackbird whistling*
> *Or just after,*

is not to speak of the initially perceived object but of an attribute one can imagine for it. Indeed, the stanza, as it echoes Keats's "Heard melodies are sweet, but those unheard/ Are sweeter," carries us out of the context of reality into the context of art in its pursuit of meaning. And finally, to ask of one's compatriots,[65]

> *O thin men of Haddam,*
> *Why do you imagine golden birds?*
> *Do you not see how the blackbird*
> *Walks around the feet*
> *Of the women about you?*

is to discard the initial perception altogether, and to make an argument for the immediate reality as opposed to the remote idea while one is in the very act of demonstrating that the artist is no more capable than the "thin men of Haddam"[66] of accepting reality as sufficient to the mind's needs. It is thus no wonder that in the eleventh stanza the poet riding over Connecticut in the glass coach of his art[67] is pierced by fear when he mistakes "The shadow of his equipage/ For blackbirds." Those shadows, the images his art constructs, are for human purposes at least the only reality the blackbird can enjoy.

The closing stanza, whose method is that of the Chinese painter, returns to the blackbird as object. But, as if the obstacles to knowledge were not already sufficiently complex, it is no longer quite the same object. Reality is in time and in motion, and the "real" blackbird, like its metaphoric counterparts, has long flown from the "twenty snowy mountains" against which he was first perceived:

> *It was evening all afternoon.*
> *It was snowing*
> *And it was going to snow.*
> *The blackbird sat*
> *In the cedar limbs.*

Surely the new images of darkness and snow in themselves deny the possibility of Pearce's unwarrantably single-minded reading, for they are projections of the mind's own bafflement and defeat, of its recognition that there is no light and no form but what the mind itself imposes. The final stanza is not the kind of close that Yeats compared to the click of a box's lid. It cannot be because it is no close, no resolution at all. The blackbird posed for thirteen portraits and could pose for thirteen or one hundred and thirty more, without yielding to the artist that essential reality, the "irreducible X," which cannot be captured because it exists only in itself and eludes the nets of poetic form one seeks to impose on it. Although "Thirteen Ways of Looking at a Blackbird," in the intricate texture of meaning and music it evokes from its subject, is an artistic triumph, it is also the record of a metaphysical defeat. What Frank Kermode said of Arnold applies (slightly edited) with equal truth to Stevens: he was tortured by the "brevity of those moments of imaginative perception he was always seeking to recapture."[68]

We may bring to at least a tenuous conclusion this account of the hazards of mimetic art and the obstacles that stand against its achievement by posing, as one must constantly pose in a discussion of Stevens, a paradox. As Stevens remarks in "Three Academic Pieces," "Poetry is a satisfying of the desire for resemblance,"[69] and thus metaphor serves not a decorative function but is the very essence of the poetic act. But poetry also stems from the desire to come to terms with things as they are, and things as they are do not partake of the universal harmony that the mind, in its hunger for ultimate resemblance, seeks to ascribe to them. Given this fact, to confine one's attention only to things as they are, although a possibility of perceptual experience, is not a possibility of art. If it were, the first stanza of "Thirteen Ways of Looking at a Blackbird" would be, as I suggested a moment ago, as far as the poem could go.

Stevens does offer, in "Metaphors of a Magnifico,"[70] an extended attempt to confine a poem solely to its root perception; and the attempt, although not the poem, is a failure. The perceived object, the thing in itself, is here represented by "Twenty men crossing a bridge," as in

"Thirteen Ways" it was represented by the bird's moving eye. The mind is this time more consciously resolved to forego the pleasure of metaphor, and to confine itself to the unembellished fact at hand. Yet the demands of predication, as well as those of thought itself, force it to seek in the fact some pattern for which it may stand. Thus the men crossing a bridge become "twenty men crossing twenty bridges,/ Into twenty villages,/ Or one man/ Crossing a single bridge into a village." These analogies, however, although abstractly true, are intractable to poetry, comprising as they do "old song/ That will not declare itself. . . ."

Thus the poem, which is a poem of process, not a reported conclusion, begins anew; now the

> *Twenty men crossing a bridge,*
> *Into a village,*
> *Are*
> *Twenty men crossing a bridge*
> *Into a village.*

The brilliantly manipulated hesitation following "are" suggests the mind's reluctance to move to a conclusion that puts mind out of work, a conclusion which once more "will not declare itself," though it "is certain as meaning." Speculative truth that confines itself to the irreducible certainty can move no further than to tautology. Naked fact shares with naked truth a barrenness and sterility that are paralyzing to the mind. To release that paralysis, the mind is virtually forced to relax its attention on the single static fact. It must give itself once more to the world of things in time, and of things that cannot be defined in themselves but only in connection with the multiplicity of other things that provide a perceptual context. Thus the flux of experience is allowed to resume its flow:

Thirteen Ways

The boots of the men clump
On the boards of the bridge.
The first white wall of the village
Rises through fruit-trees.
Of what was I thinking?
So the meaning escapes.

The imagination has won the indulgence it demands,
but as the starkness of the opening lines gives over to
the sound and color and variegated form of the stanza
just quoted, the pleasures of perception are won at the
cost of meaning. We have turned from the irreducible
men to the clump of their boots, to the boards of the
bridge, the white wall, and the village itself rising
through fruit trees. Yet the poem closes not in celebration over the recovery of color, sound, and motion, but
in bewilderment over the failure to achieve meaning
by stopping time. The poem closes with two final,
futile gestures to anchor itself to the single, static perception:

> *The first wall of the village . . .*
> *The fruit-trees . . .*

But, were the wall or the trees now to be taken for
new subject, precisely the same process would take
place. Ultimate meaning is irreconcilable with the
perceptual process; the poem cannot stop time, but can
only reflect the tension between the mind's desire to do
so and the senses' refusal to comply.[71]

To the question I raised earlier in this chapter—is it
possible for art to mirror without distorting reality—
we have seen that the answer is no. Insofar as art imposes its own form on reality, it must, whatever its intent, distort that which it reflects. If, as in "Anecdote of
the Jar," the poem successfully imposes on reality a

rigid pattern around which it may be ordered, the resulting composition will be sterile and barren, and therefore unreal. And if, as in "Metaphors of a Magnifico," the poem returns to the perceptual flux, art is still as far from reality, although the distance must now be measured in a different direction. Art that moves in time may, as it were, give a true impression of the river, but it is forced to forego an examination of each of the constituent drops. An art that confines itself to representing things as they are is confronted, first, by "the irreducible X" that is always outside the confines of art; and second, by the awareness that only the shaping imagination can provide reality with pattern and meaning. On the other hand, art that confines itself solely to the imagination's desire for pleasurable harmony may be achieved only at the price of exile from the world. Deprived of the objective reality which, by metamorphosis, the imagination attempts to make adequate to its desire, the imagination must suffer the aridity that ultimately drives the poet's soul, as in Tennyson's "Palace of Art," back into the world.

I have emphasized in this chapter Stevens' sensitivity to the arguments that may be leveled against poetry. Among them is one whose truth he was forced to acknowledge: that art in fact cannot mirror reality. From that concession, however, stems a further claim: poetry can provide not only a vision of reality but also a precise means of demonstrating how, to the human observer, the version of reality provided by the imagination, despite the arbitrariness of its form, is no more a distortion than versions limited to the findings of the sense and reason. The poetic version of reality, however, is not merely as "true" as other versions. Because it represents and teaches us to seek "the good in what is harmonious and orderly," it represents also the means by which we can find pleasure in the play of the mind and discover the varied music inherent in the smallest fragment of sensual experience. For Stevens as for Blake, a grain of sand is first a grain of sand, a wild flower first a wild flower, the eye of a blackbird first the eye of a blackbird. But the value of these things depends on the way we choose to perceive them. As objects to which we respond only through sense and reason, they are lifeless pieces of data. As objects whose complexity of form and interrelationship it is the imagination's delight to explore, they are indeed the eternities and heavens that Blake found them to be.

Stevens lived in an age still more rationalistic than Blake's, and, further removed than Blake from a viable religious tradition, Stevens could no longer make his case for poetic vision in the spiritual terms that were still potent when Blake used them. Granting all this, and granting too the sometimes destructive sense of irony that Stevens unavoidably shared with the poets of his time, he, no less than Blake, believed it within the power of the poet, and through the poet, of his readers,

> To open the Eternal Worlds, to open the immortal
> Eyes
> Of Man inwards into the Worlds of Thought, into
> Eternity
> Ever expanding in the Bosom of God, the Human
> Imagination.[72]

VI

The Longest Journey

We observed in the preceding chapter that the world of *Harmonium* is far less narrowly a hedonistic world than critics most frequently argue it to be. Throughout the volume we are in the company not of a mind wallowing in the free pleasures of the imagination and senses, but rather of a mind laboring to carve from its intractable environment an aesthetic sufficiently "tough, diverse, untamed"[1] to teach us the possibility and desirability of such pleasures, to guide us toward discovering anew the color and multifold play of experience still available to us in a post-Darwinian world.

Because Stevens inevitably shared some of the prevailing rationalism of that world, he shared also some of the skepticism with which it viewed the imagination's claims. Unable, then, to give himself freely to the pure play of the imagination, Stevens seems to have been determined to market in his poetry only a product he had rigorously pretested against the frictions of reality, a product he could stand behind solidly, and the proof of whose value he could readily produce for anyone sufficiently interested to question it. However, the very fact that we live in a world in which not many are so interested itself must raise a new kind of friction. In confronting the forces marshaled against the poet in our time, Stevens was concerned not only with those threats that issue from the nature of poetry and the imagination themselves, but also with the conflict between the very fabric of modern society and the imagination's thirst for aggrandizement.

We may best approach this new question by first pausing to call attention to the aesthetic cul-de-sac in which Stevens found himself at the close of the *Harmonium* period. In October 1922, he had remarked in a letter to Harriet Monroe: "Gathering together the things for my book makes me wonder at *Poetry's* friendliness. . . . [The] reading of these outmoded and debilitated poems [makes] me wish rather desperately to keep on dabbling and to be as obscure as possible until I have perfected an authentic and fluent speech for myself."[2] Stevens had, in fact, spent the previous summer working on a long poem that recorded his struggle toward "an authentic and fluent speech." The purpose behind his desire to write a long poem, he wrote to Miss Monroe in September 1922, was "not obsequiousness to the judgment of the people" who evaluate poets by volume. "On the contrary, I find that this prolonged attention to a single subject has the same result that prolonged attention a senora [sic] has, according to the authorities. All manner of favors drop from it."[3] Yet from "The Comedian as the Letter C," the long poem he had recently finished revising, something other than favors had dropped. The "skill in the varying of the serenade" required in a long poem, he complained to Miss Monroe, "occasionally makes me feel like a Guatemalan when one wants to feel like an Italian."[4] This real, if only occasional, conviction that his own art was too crude for the subject it conveyed is certainly one of the reasons behind the strangely equivocal bad marks he assigned to "The Comedian," when, at the close of this letter, he remarked: "I expect that after a while Crispin (the present title is "The Comedian as the Letter C") will become rudimentary and abhorrent."

Despite the fact that "The Comedian" is, as Samuel French Morse describes it, "a kind of *summa poemarum* of all that precedes it,"[5] Stevens had solid reason to anticipate future dissatisfaction with it. The poem is the record of an aesthetic voyage that ends at half-circle.[6] Crispin, the poet-hero of the work who serves as Stevens' mask, discovers much in his voyaging, but his essential discovery, as we shall see, destroys the possibility of art.

The object of Crispin's voyage is to shake off "The last distortion of romance,"[7] and Crispin appears to achieve that object in the poem's first section. Beginning as a romantic solipsist who considers himself the "principium and lex" (CP, p. 27) around which the external world composes itself, Crispin hears in the disorderly magnitude of the sea "Polyphony beyond his baton's thrust" (CP, p. 28). With this initial movement toward the recognition of an external reality beyond art's power to order we have arrived at the central concern of the poem. Crispin's task is to break free from an aesthetic whose root principle is that "man is the intelligence of his soil" (CP, p. 27) and replace it with one which recognizes that "his soil is man's intelligence" (CP, p. 36). Since the first principle maintains the imagination, the second, reality, to be sovereign, we perceive that "The Comedian" is a macrocosmic dramatization of the same conflict we studied on a microcosmic scale in the preceding chapter. In "The Comedian," however, we become more clearly aware of one implication of the conflict that is suggested only tangentially by the poems we examined earlier.

One of the romantic distortions of which Crispin-Stevens was trying to purge himself was the tendency to "mythologize" reality in order to make it conform to his desire. Stevens made this point to Renato Poggioli when he wrote that "The Comedian"

> is what may be called an anti-mythological poem. The central figure is an every-day man who lives a life without the slightest adventure except that he lives it in a [corrected from "the"] poetic ["American" deleted] atmosphere as we all do. This point makes it necessary for a translator to try to reproduce the every-day plainness of the central figure and the plush, so to speak, of his stage.[8]

In carrying out these intentions, however, and freeing himself from the bondage of the falsifying imagination, Stevens was driven to a position from which the work of art no longer appeared to have metaphysical justification. The record of Crispin's voyage is in this respect a record of failure: Crispin begins in search of a new aesthetic and ends by rejecting the possibility of art.

However difficult, then, "The Comedian" may be in some of its particulars, it is impossible to agree with Frank Kermode, who finds the poem "in every sense a fantastic performance," "a narrative of obscurely allegorical intent, harsh and dream-like"; and who remarks that its manner is "a sustained nightmare of unexpected diction, so that one sometimes thinks of it less as a poem than as a remarkable physical feat."[9] The question of diction I will return to at the close of this chapter. For the present, I wish only to point out that its allegorical *intention* is precisely the aspect of "The Comedian" which is least obscure: the poem is a record of Stevens' poetic exploration and progress through the *Harmonium* period; and it traces, albeit erratically, the evolution from a youthful subjectivism to an eighteenth-century conservative realism which maintains that "For realist, what is is what should be."[10] Unfortunately for Crispin's poems, however, that last doctrine destroyed the possibility of poetry by destroying the conflict between "is" and "ought to be" that we have seen to comprise the dialectic from which the poem springs. Crispin does not, therefore, abandon poetry *as a result* of the marriage and the raising of a family celebrated in the closing two sections of the poem. His domestication, whether we read it on a literal or an allegorical level, is effect, not cause. He settled down only after he, "as realist, admitted that"

> *Whoever haunts a matinal continent*
> *May, after all, stop before a plum*
> *And be content and still be realist.*
> *The words of things entangle and confuse.*
> *The plum survives its poems. It may hang*
> *In the sunshine placidly, colored by ground*
> *Obliquities of those who pass beneath,*
> *Harlequined and mazily dewed and mauved*
> *In bloom. Yet it survives in its own form,*
> *Beyond those changes, good, fat, guzzly fruit.*
> *So Crispin hasped on the surviving form*
> *For him, of shall or ought to be in is.*[11]

It is impossible to read these lines, which constitute so explicit a renunciation of poetry, in isolation from the fact that they were written at precisely the time when Stevens was about to move into a period of long silence. More interesting, however, than the fact that "The Comedian" ends—I feel certain it did not so begin—as a farewell to poetry are the reasons for the fact. One of these reasons is stated in the passage quoted above. Stevens had concluded that poetry must inevitably distort its object. The poets who stand beneath the real plum, however they color it with their art, render it "Harlequined and mazily dewed and mauved/ In bloom," succeed only in entangling and confusing its reality. Their art can neither capture nor even touch the plum's essential form, that "irreducible X" which rests always outside the margins of art. Unwilling to content himself with counterfeit, and unable to convince himself that art mints true coin, Stevens had for the moment cut himself off from the possibility of providing a metaphysical justification for poetry.

Since, however, Stevens had been haunted throughout the *Harmonium* period by this same fear that art could be no more than decoration, his new statement of the fear cannot in itself explain the note of renunciation and defeat, albeit relieved by gaiety of language, that marks the close of "The Comedian." We discover, in fact, that to his chronic misgiving a new factor now lent support. He had discovered, ironically, that the satisfaction with life itself which Crispin experiences through his domestication were destructive to the appetites that lead to creation. As he observed in the penultimate section of the poem,

> . . . the quotidian saps philosophers
> And men like Crispin like them in intent,
> If not in will, to track the knaves of thought.[12]

Thus Crispin's new contentment with the round of quotidian experience, although a round comprised "Of breakfast ribands, fruit laid in their leaves" (*CP*, p. 42), and other richness of flower and birdsong and love—even this routine of life at its most pleasurable best, proves in the end to sap "like the sun" (*CP*, p. 43).

The willingness of the domesticated Crispin to

forego the "shall or ought to be" out of contentment with the "is" (*CP*, p. 41) will hardly seem to us the "haphazard denouement" it seemed to him (*CP*, p. 40). As I have said, the dialectical conflict we have seen to be the wellspring of Stevens' art requires, for its survival, an energetic discontent. For Stevens, perhaps for all creators, the creative process struggles to bring what is more closely in harmony with envisioned perfection. Crispin's life history thus teaches us one of life's nicer absurdities: that the contented man has lost the need to make songs. Having achieved the stasis of contentment, was Crispin

> . . . *to bray this in profoundest brass*
> *Arointing his dreams with fugal requiems?*
> *Was he to company vastest things defunct*
> *With a blubber of tom-toms harrowing the sky?*
> *Scrawl a tragedian's testament? Prolong*
> *His active force in an inactive dirge,*
> *Which, let the tall musicians call and call,*
> *Should merely call him dead? Pronounce amen*
> *Through choirs infolded to the utmost clouds?*
> *Because he built a cabin who once planned*
> *Loquacious columns by the ructive sea?*[13]

No, just as in these lines Crispin ironically accepts his poetic death, so this poem must have seemed to Stevens as he completed it a last poetic testament.

Now that we have established the nature of the poetic cul-de-sac into which Stevens had driven himself in the early twenties, it will be useful to trace the aesthetic steps through which he moved en route to this apparently final position. These steps are of particular interest because, first, they reveal to us what Stevens considered to be the aesthetic alternatives open to the American poet at this time; and second, because these same alternatives, as varied and even as contradictory as they are, would be reestablished in a state of uneasy coexistence when Stevens returned to poetry in the thirties. In terms of this second point, Stevens' use of the voyage-quest structure is misleading. Although Crispin considers each of his newly discovered poetic creeds to be truer, more "realistic," than the last, the ultimate failure of any of them to sustain him makes clear that he was mistaken. Each attempt at formulating the ultimate, definitive aesthetic doctrine produces only another part of that whole which, fortunately for his poetry if not for his theory, Stevens was never to bring to final harmony. "The Comedian" is an early manifestation of a longing that remained with Stevens late—in terms of Isaiah Berlin's famous metaphor, the longing of the fox to be a hedgehog.

The aesthetic point of embarkation from which Crispin sets sail is stated in the poem's first line: "Nota: man is the intelligence of his soil."[14] This precept is one we have seen in practice before, in those poems which suggest that whatever order or meaning the artist may "discover" in the external world is the order of meaning he invents. Crispin's release from solipsism is effected by means of a sea-cure. It is an easy enough matter, he comes to realize, to be "the Socrates/ Of snails, musician of pears" (CP, p. 27), and such apparently tidy and malleable terrestrial objects as these. But Crispin discovers that the sea is not to be pent within any facile structure of art; its polyphony is "beyond his baton's thrust" (CP, p. 28). Unable to maintain his subjectivist hybris against the pressure of protean magnitude, Crispin can no longer find satisfaction in the minor poetry he once wrote; but neither is he yet prepared to provide the major treatment demanded by his newly expanded sense of reality.

Nor does Crispin's release from a comfortable anthropocentricity entail only a change in perceptual and poetic habits; it also entails a reappraisal of self. The new Crispin, humbled and stripped of self-delusion, "A skinny sailor peering in the sea-glass" (*CP*, p. 28), is no more than an apprentice to reality, a valet to the world. Yet he has managed at least to cast off the "old mythology of self," and can look back at the old Crispin,

> The lutanist of fleas, the knave, the thane,
> The ribboned stick, the bellowing breeches, cloak
> Of China, cap of Spain, imperative haw
> Of hum, inquisitorial botanist,
> And general lexicographer of mute
> And maidenly greenhorns,[15]

as a pretentious and ridiculous figure, a poet decked out in archaic and comically exotic regalia. It seems clear that the mythologies of self "blotched out beyond unblotching" in this process of self-revelation are not, as Hi Simons argues, Crispin's "imagination of himself in a multiplicity of god-like roles"[16] so much as they are his old poetic costumes, the exotic but conventional singing robes that now appear outmoded and ridiculous, just as Iffucan's costume and swaggering air appeared ridiculous to the Inchling. Stripped of all artifice, freed from the modes by which he had distorted his own and the world's realities, Crispin at this stage in his voyage resembles the listener in "The Snowman," who, "nothing himself, beholds/ Nothing that is not there and the nothing that is."[17]

At this first stage in his journey, Crispin has achieved a kind of realism: "The last distortion of romance/ Forsook the insatiable egotist."[18] Hi Simons has remarked that it "is a realism without positive content, consisting merely in recognizing the stark realities of life."[19] But the question is not so much of stark realities as of realities whose meaning and form sprawl beyond any structure we may erect to contain them. Although such awareness may represent a significant advance toward truth, it requires that a considerable price be paid by art. Stevens was not yet prepared to discover how poetry could be made, without the distortion of romance, from the sea. That task he would accomplish nearly twelve years later in "The Idea of Order at Key West."[20] At this earlier moment, however, although Crispin is certain that in the sea he has confronted "the veritable ding an sich," "a vocable thing," he is aware too that the speech it belches "out of hoary darks" no way resembles his.[21] For the time being, then, any poem he might make would be an evasion: "here was no help before reality" (*CP*, p. 30). Sadly, as the title of the first section announces, reality is equivalent to "The World without Imagination," and thus no more lends itself to art than will the "Nice Shady Home" in which the finally domesticated Crispin will later take up residence. The sea has taught Crispin new faith in "the strict austerity/ Of one vast, subjugating, final tone" (*CP*, p. 30). Now his task as artist is the discovery of a human style that may adequately represent the non-human ultimate reality, the lineaments of the supreme fiction he has seen manifest in the sea's wild form and heard articulate in the sea's voice.

The second stage in Crispin's journey, described in the section entitled "Concerning the Thunderstorms of Yucatan," is more complex in matter, apparently less certain in direction, than the first. Whereas in "The World without Imagination" individual details are subordinated to the overriding purgatorial theme, the second section presents a multiplicity of experiences and doctrines that are neither structured against any comprehensive pattern nor individually developed beyond what in several cases is no more than brief notation. Of the two possible explanations for the looser structure and more opaque meaning of the second part, I do not know which to prefer. On the one hand, it may be argued, Stevens ran into the same kind of difficulty that Blake encountered in the Prophetic Books. Both poets were dealing with subjects requiring more precise discrimination than a pure allegorical form allows, and both poets lacked the dramatic sense that the literal level of effective allegory requires. As a result, "The Comedian," like Blake's visionary work, is continually threatened by a breakdown on the literal level under the pressure of the poet's far more intense preoccupation with the symbolic level. On the other hand, it may be argued that the less organic structure of the second section is appropriate to its theme. Whereas Crispin at sea is exposed to "the strict austerity/ Of one vast, subjugating, final tone," Crispin in the tropical jungles confronts a luxuriant, chaotic growth which creates desire for but does not reveal "beautiful barenesses as yet unseen."[22] Viewed in this framework, the structure of each of these sections mirrors its theme.

Having granted the difficulties of the Yucatan section, let us determine how far the reader can surmount them. The voyager who disembarks in Yucatan, a tropical, luxuriant setting of the kind that dominates the environment of *Harmonium,* is, as Stevens calls him, a freeman.[23] Crispin has cast off "the last distortion of romance" and is thus free in the sense that Stevens defines in "Imagination as Value," when he remarks that "The imagination is the liberty of the mind. The romantic is a failure to make use of that liberty."[24] Crispin has been purged of delusion, and now, destitute, he seeks new clothes, experience, and knowledge compatible with the reality-principle he has learned at sea. He rejects out of hand the model offered by the Maya sonneteers, romantic platonists who, like the "thin men of Haddam," ignore the real birds around them in order to make pleas to "the night-bird," an illusionary ideal. Yet, although Crispin rejects their solution, he is confronted by the same problem as they. The real beauty of "raspberry tanagers in palms,/ High up in orange air" is as inadequate to his needs as to theirs, not because he like them finds that beauty "barbarous," but because "Crispin was too destitute to find/ In any commonplace the sought-for aid."[25] Driven therefore more deeply into the exotic jungle of reality, "His violence . . . for aggrandizement/ And not for stupor," Crispin pursues "an aesthetic tough, diverse, untamed,/ Green barbarism turning paradigm" (*CP*, p. 31)—the kind of aesthetic we saw hinted at in "Floral Decorations for Bananas." It is apparent that what Crispin and Stevens were seeking is a poetic style capable of conveying the exotic fecundity of nature by means of a language that did not distort by superimposing an opulence of its own.

The jungles of Yucatan, I may now suggest, are, like the sea, symbolic of an ultimate reality, a "veritable ding an sich." But the sea is equated with winter, and therefore the north: it is a reality ultimately stark, and reduces Crispin to a state in which "nothing of himself/ Remained, except some starker, barer self/ In a starker, barer world . . . (*CP*, p. 29). It is a reality which, without imaginative aggrandizement, is intractable to poetry. On the contrary, the jungle, southern, fecund, multifarious, creates desire for but will not reveal "beautiful barenesses," out of which Crispin might forge the intrinsic verse of the fabulous. Instead, it is smothering, over-lush, and forces Crispin to concede

That earth was like a jostling festival
Of seeds grown fat, too juicily opulent
Expanding in the gold's maternal warmth.[26]

Crispin has thus undergone two contrary processes: the first a stripping away of stale mannerisms and false modes of perception, the second a building up of new sensual experience. Each movement has provided him with a vision of a possible aesthetic, but neither, in the end, has made it possible for him to write verse. Thus, despite his frequent cries of triumph, he is not, as artist, better off than he had been before his journey began, when he "wrote his couplet yearly to the spring." (CP, p. 31).

The second section ends with the thunderstorm referred to in its title, but once more, whatever the storm teaches Crispin of self and reality, it merely foreshadows rather than provides new dimensions to his art. Stevens, whom Robert Frost once accused, with partial truth, of writing about bric-a-brac rather than subjects, lends some support to the charge, at least as it applies to his early work, with his account of Crispin's response to the thunder. In it Crispin hears something harsher than he had known before, and it provides him with a new paradigm: "the span/ Of force, the quintessential fact, the note/ Of Vulcan, that a valet seeks to own."[27] Yet, although the voice of the thunder fills Crispin with elation, intensity, and profundity, and provides him, "lapsing in its clap," with "gigantic quavers of its voice,/ For Crispin to vociferate again," we are compelled to take these statements on faith, since the gigantic quavers leave no echoes in the verse describing the scene.

The first two sections of "The Comedian," as we have seen, are an allegorical account of a poet's attempt to remake himself. Self-exiled from an environment that is no longer poetically nourishing, he has entered a regimen of therapy, expanding his vision by confronting first, reality at its most austere, and second, reality at its most opulent. From each confrontation he has learned the possibility of new poetic modes superior to that which he had practiced in his own early work, when his sense of reality was pallid and conventional, and he lived in a world in which the sun "shone/ With bland complaisance on pale parasols" (*CP*, p. 29). Crispin has in effect spent his forty days in the desert; his next step must be to apply what he has learned there to the environment from which he sailed.

Thus, in "Approaching Carolina," the third section of the poem, Crispin prepares for his return to America. The section in many respects resembles "Farewell to Florida," a poem in which, fourteen years later, Stevens was to relive the basic struggles he recorded in "The Comedian." Both poems are concerned with the poet's determination, at once exultant and bitter, to abandon an environment that attracts him because it provides in reality the opulence the imagination craves. At the same time, however, Stevens was already aware by the time he wrote the earlier poem that the life of his poetry required dialectical opposition between reality and imagination; and from that point of view, engagement with "the vulgar" as theme (*CP*, p. 33) could in the end be more rewarding than the celebration of the opulent, in the end lend to his poetry that "span of force" he had heard in the thunder and sought to echo in his verse. The voyage north, then, is an attempt to come to terms with the texture of contemporary reality by applying to it the relatively abstract lessons he had learned through sea and jungle.

Behind this intention, however, there is a power-

ful ambivalence that may appear baffling, baffling because Stevens has encouraged the reader to expect that
Crispin is in fact passing through a progressive philosophical evolution from romantic ironist to realist. Unquestionably, to trace such an evolution was Stevens' conscious intent. But how are we to reconcile that intention
with the fact that the same Crispin who has abandoned
"the last distortion of romance" (CP, p. 30) regresses,
at the opening of the third section, to dependence on the
old moonlight fictions? Surely the unwritten book of
moonlight in whose pages Stevens demands that a place
be found for Crispin is the history of the romantic imagination. The problem, of course, is that while the non-
human realities of sea and jungle could be confronted
without the distortions of romance, the human, social
reality of contemporary society could not be. The America that Crispin prepares to confront is itself a place
unreal:

> America was always north to him,
> A northern west or western north, but north,
> And thereby polar, polar-purple, chilled
> And lank, rising and slumping from a sea
> Of hardy foam, receding flatly, spread
> In endless ledges, glittering, submerged
> And cold in a boreal mistiness of the moon.[28]

A polar, misty continent, its spring still frosty, its summer "wet, not ripening," its winter vacant, its dominant
colors purple and blue-black, America is "Morose
chiaroscuro, gauntly drawn" (CP, p. 34). Crispin's desire to achieve a "blissful liaison" between himself and
so forbidding an environment entailed a forbidding task
indeed; and it is thus no wonder that Crispin is forced,
"In his observant progress," to deny himself many
poems, "lesser things/ Than the relentless contact he
desired."[29]

In terms of the light it casts on the total body of Stevens' work, I should consider "Approaching Carolina" to be the crucial section of "The Comedian." Stevens had begun the poem by repudiating the earlier work of the *Harmonium* period as alien to his native soil (the old Crispin wore outlandish costumes of China and Spain, and initially set sail from Bordeaux, presumably symbolic of the French *symboliste* tradition that was one of Stevens' poetic sources). In his search for a new and authentic style, Stevens had developed two paradigms to which his art might aspire: first, from the sea, "the strict austerity/ Of one vast, subjugating, final tone," and second, from the jungle, the conviction that the fabulous has its seat in reality in itself, not in the imagination's embellishments of reality. Such lessons as these, however, can have value only in their application, only insofar as they may make possible a poetic mode that seeks beauty not through reaction against one's world but rather through direct and fastidious confrontation of it. At bottom, then, the task before Crispin is to invent and perfect a truly native American poetry that can at once satisfy the imagination's craving for the fabulous and the reality-principle's insistence on an undistorted vision of things as they are.

With characteristically fastidious honesty, however, Stevens was forced to concede that contemporary American reality, pervaded by "Arctic moonlight," itself appeared to be an evasion of that ultimate reality he sought: "It seemed/ Illusive, faint, more mist than moon, perverse,/ Wrong as a divagation to Peking."[30] The position at which he had arrived, then, despite his insistence that his theme was to be vulgar and that moonlight was an evasion, was not that of relentless realist but rather of poetic dialectician, who

> . . . *conceived his voyaging to be*
> *An up and down between two elements,*
> *A fluctuating between sun and moon,*
> *A sally into gold and crimson forms,*
> *As on this voyage, out of goblinry,*
> *And then retirement like a turning back*
> *And sinking down to the indulgences*
> *That in the moonlight have their habitude.*[31]

As the outline of a poetic itinerary to which he would not again return for nearly a decade, this passage was to prove remarkably prescient. The fluctuation between sun and moon was indeed to set the pattern for all Stevens' subsequent work; and these symbols, we should note here, operate not simply in their conventional senses of reality and imagination, but also, against the backdrop of the sun-drenched tropics and the moon-lit North, as symbols of the reality of opulence vs. the reality of the austere.

"Approaching Carolina" appears to end in triumph, as Crispin, savoring rankness like a sensualist," sees in the land to which he had returned "how much/ Of what he saw he never saw at all," and grips finally, through his direct confrontation with the vulgar, "the essential prose," the one integrity "in a world so falsified" (CP, p. 36). Yet this apparent reconciliation with America is qualified by the fact that it is not really to America that Crispin returns. The voyager, who requires "For his refreshment" a flourishing tropic whose harmony was barbaric, undefined, returns not to contemporary reality but to "a Carolina of old time,/ A little juvenile, an ancient whim . . ." (CP, p. 35). It is the American South, historically and in the context of Stevens' geographical symbolism, identified with the past, itself an evasion of the polar America, the "morose chiaroscuro, gauntly drawn," that he had resolved to face.

As clearly as I can determine from the admittedly difficult passage on which I have been commenting, Crispin has averted rather than resolved the conflicts he had anticipated in achieving liaison with his environment; and it is only thus that at the beginning of the fourth section of the poem he is able to lay bare "in one laconic phrase" the doctrine he had been questing after: "Nota: his soil is man's intelligence" (*CP*, p. 36). He who began as a self-deluded petty tyrant over the snails and fleas to whom his mind alone—so he believed —could give meaning, is ready now to rediscover his proper relationship with his environment, a relationship that will aggrandize instead of diminishing both the inhabitant and the world he inhabits, and which will achieve this aggrandizement independently of the distortions of romance. Crispin has rediscovered America, a new-found land, because he has disciplined himself to see it newly. The fruit he anticipates will ripen on the vines of this new perception is not simply a new mode of poetry—or, more precisely, "prose/ More exquisite than any tumbling verse" (*CP*, p. 37). More important, it is a new society of men who, like Crispin, no longer find nourishment in traditional and stale modes of perception and thought, and who will learn with him to experience their environment as vital and new-born. Nowhere in the poem does the note of triumphant revelation ring out more boldly than here:

> *What was the purpose of his pilgrimage,*
> *Whatever shape it took in Crispin's mind,*
> *If not, when all is said, to drive away*
> *The shadow of his fellows from the skies,*
> *And from their stale intelligence released,*
> *To make a new intelligence prevail?*[32]

Crispin's apprenticeship is over. Turning from "The torment of fastidious thought grown slack" to a "bellicose" utopianism (*CP*, p. 37), he plans a colony of men who live in blissful harmony with their environment. Made up of individuals who through art may speak separately for their diverse regions and celebrate, on native instruments, the birds, flowers, and fruit that comprise the reality indigenous to their regions, such a colony could achieve, communally, what the individual artist cannot achieve individually. What Stevens had in mind here is not, of course, a literal artists' colony. He was rather contemplating a sense of artistic community through which the work of each poet would color and be colored by the work of all. As a collection of individuals, the imagined colony would represent the multitudinous harmonies of man and region that no single individual could contain separately; and as community, the colony itself would constitute the unity behind this opulent diversity.

Here the total conception Crispin has pursued since his sea-baptism appears to be realized; he has found a means "to make whole among/ The ruses that were shattered by the large" (*CP*, p. 30). But it is at this point that with an astounding although hardly unprecedented reversal Crispin rejects his idea of a colony in almost the same breath with which he formulates it:

> *These bland excursions into time to come,*
> *Related in romance to backward flights,*
> *However prodigal, however proud,*
> *Contained in their afflatus the reproach*
> *That first drove Crispin to his wandering.*[33]

He sees the colony as another "counterfeit," another "masquerade of thought," by which the challenges that reality issues to the poet may be averted, by which complexities and contradictions may be reduced to alluringly tidy order, and, most dangerously, by which the poet himself would be legislated against "With fictive flourishes that preordained/ His passion's permit, hang of coat, degree/ Of buttons, measure of his salt" (*CP,* p. 39). Thus, for the last time, Crispin again chooses text over gloss, reality over the orders the mind seeks to impose on it. The choice brings his aesthetic pilgrimage virtually to an end; there remains only to accomplish his reacclimatization to things as they are, and with that reacclimatization, a philosophic and sensual contentment that precludes the need for art.

Two inharmonious points should now be clear: first, Stevens was frequently driven by the same procrustean impulses to which his critics have often succumbed; and second, for all his rage for order he was curiously obsessed with truth. Surely that obsession, as it manifests itself in "The Comedian," *is* curious. It compelled Stevens to write a poem that does not, as he desired, record a poet's progress toward the resolution of the conflicts that obsessed him. Instead, Crispin's repeated triumphs are the triumphs of Sisyphus, and each section of "The Comedian" records the laborious rolling of an immense boulder to the rim of the hill from which it immediately rolls back down.

Neither the exigencies of poetic form nor the craving of his imagination could put to rest Stevens' chronic distrust of finality. Thus, his remarkable renunciation of the idea of a colony was in a sense inevitable; it is simply part of the pattern he had established in the third section, when "he conceived his voyaging to be/ An up and down between two elements,/ A fluctuating between sun and moon" (*CP,* p. 35). On the other hand, given Stevens' insistence on that pattern of fluctuation, there was good reason, even in 1922, to surmise that Crispin's renunciation of dreams and indeed of poetry itself would not constitute Stevens' last word. If, as Crispin insisted, dreams chain us to the past instead of freeing us for a future, if they are "the heirs/ Of dreamers buried in our sleep, and not/ The oncoming fantasies of better birth" (CP, p. 39), Stevens would nevertheless reaffirm their necessity when he attempted to impose "Ideas of Order" on the chaos of the thirties.

We have returned to our point of departure. Purged of discontent, Crispin has become a Popean realist, for whom "what is is what should be" (CP, p. 41). Resigned to the belief that "The words of things entangle and confuse./ The plum survives its poems" (CP, p. 41), he has renounced art, and in a sense thought itself, in favor of the living experience that is the raw material of art and thought. Unable to maintain his larger conception of a communal sensibility of new men, he has made for himself a private one of wife and four daughters. Thus, whatever truths Crispin was able to pluck in the course of his travels can no longer have use for him, since the questions that drove him to them have been laid to rest. His daughters, "four blithe instruments/ Of differing struts," have displaced his poems, and through them he hears "sounds of music coming to accord/ Upon his lap" (CP, p. 45). Thus it is that "the quotidian saps philosophers." Crispin's voyage ends, not really in triumph or defeat, but in a state of physical and mental contentment that makes irrelevant such triumphs or defeats.

"The Comedian" has frequently been used as evidence for critical indictment of Stevens. For Julian Symons the poem "remains a piece of virtuosity, a literary curio."[34] J. V. Cunningham discusses it, in his brilliantly hostile essay, as part of his demonstration that Stevens' attempt to replace traditional religious myths with secular ones was doomed to artistic and philosophic failure.[35] And even Roy Harvey Pearce, one of Stevens' most sympathetic and illuminating critics, describes "The Comedian" as "the most difficult, most ambitious, and, I think, most inadequate of the poems in *Harmonium*," and complains that "its technique is of a kind which can only inhibit the emergence of [its] meaning."[36]

Whether or not the poem is the artistic failure that Pearce considers it to be must of course remain a question of taste. Yet several of the difficulties that stand in the way of readers who may wish to settle that question for themselves can be surmounted. First, as I have already demonstrated, to read the poem with the expectation of consistent logical evolution is to guarantee one's bewilderment; its pattern is fluctuating, a fluctuation between sun and moon. Second, to assume that because the poem is *about* an aesthetic failure it must be one is equivalent to arguing that *Hamlet* is a dramatic failure because it is about an imperfect man. Third, to suggest, as Pearce does, that the poem is obscure because "Particulars get in the way of implicit generalizations"[37] is not so much to miss the point as to appropriate one of the poem's own arguments and turn it into a criticism of the poem. What Pearce considers a technical weakness *is* in fact an implicit generalization which is stated *explicitly* more than once in the poem—as, for example, in the line, "The plum survives its poems," or again, more complexly:

> *Hence the reverberations in the words*
> *Of his first central hymns, the celebrant*
> *Of rankest trivia, tests of the strength*
> *Of his aesthetic, his philosophy,*
> *The more invidious, the more desired. . . .*[38]

Crudely translated, the first statement insists that the plum as object is more "real" than any poem (or any generalization) we may weave around it; while the second demands that the test of any viable aesthetic is its ability to come to terms with the particular.

My fourth point, I believe, comes closest to explaining what has prevented so consummately brilliant a bravura piece as "The Comedian" from taking its place with the handful of acknowledged poetic masterpieces of our age. I refer to the refusal of Stevens' language to be serious. We take no offense at the ironies of John Crowe Ransom because they so explicitly reflect his refusal to aspire to majority. We are likewise untroubled when Yeats describes himself as "a comfortable kind of old scarecrow" because his warranted confidence in his own greatness is solid enough to make his self-ironies read like Socrates' confessions of ignorance. But Stevens' case is different. First, because he really *does* see something comically pretentious in his own quest for an ultimate aesthetic; and second, because his heady euphuism —or, to borrow Hazlitt's term, his verbal "gusto"—seems at times to militate against meaning altogether. "The Comedian," as anyone who studies it soon becomes aware, cannot be read without the aid of an unabridged dictionary, and some of its most puzzling words, as Hi Simons discovered, are technical legal terms[39] which it must have amused Stevens to put to work in such alien company. Yet I confess that "The Comedian" contains some—not, I think, many—passages that not all the dictionaries in the world could render translatable, as for instance the one in which Stevens remarks that "the quotidian"

> Like this, saps like the sun, true fortuner.
> For all it takes it gives a humped return
> Exchequering from piebald fiscs unkeyed.[40]

It is difficult to believe that Stevens' tongue was anywhere but in his cheek when in a letter to Renato
Poggioli he expressed doubt over the possibility of translating the last line of the quoted passage in such a way
as "to preserve anything except the sense of the words."[41]
One would assume that for the translator sense would
pose far greater difficulty than sound; surely, this side
of Hopkins, that "humped return" and the last line
entire are something new under the sun.

I do not believe with Blackmur and others that
Stevens' diction, particularly when it is carried to the
exotic extremes common in "The Comedian," can be
explained simply in terms of the poet's quest for the
right word.[42] A more adequate explanation can be
reached by observing that Stevens, no less than Keats,
looked "upon fine Phrases like a Lover," and by tracing
the implications of the fact. Principal among these implications, it seems to me, is that in Stevens' aesthetics,
just as the poem may be a heterocosm, a "second nature"
related to but not simply mirroring reality, so may the
poem's language be a heterocosmic version of the poem
itself.[43]

That Stevens did see a connection between our
habits of diction and the way we view the world can
easily be demonstrated. In "The Noble Rider and the
Sound of Words," for instance, after commenting on
the "spirit of negation" that presides over our age,
Stevens remarked, with only apparent irrelevance, that
"We pick up the radio and find that comedians regard
the public use of words of more than two syllables as
funny."[44] Still more germane is this passage in "Three
Academic Pieces":

> If the desire for resemblance is the desire to enjoy
> reality, it may be no less true that the desire to
> enjoy reality, an acute enough desire today, is the

desire for elegance. Euphuism had its origin in the desire for elegance and it was euphuism that was a reason in the sun for metaphor.[45]

Since one of the intended goals of Crispin's voyage was to discover the possibility of delight in contemporary reality, we can infer from this passage that the primary intention of the euphuistic diction of "The Comedian" was to recover, through words, some of that enjoyment of reality to which newly coined, mouth-filling words gave expression in the earlier Elizabethan period, when the richness of language went hand in hand with the excitement of new experiential and aesthetic discovery. In the twentieth century, however, such a device is necessarily a makeshift by which one part of a world response is used to evoke the whole. Ultimately, it was as a makeshift that Stevens himself saw it: euphuistic language, like the romantic imagination itself, was one more of those distortions of reality of which he was attempting to purge his art:

> He could not be content with counterfeit,
> With masquerade of thought, with hapless words
> That must belie the racking masquerade,
> With fictive flourishes that preordained
> His passion's permit, hang of coat, degree
> Of buttons, measure of his salt. Such trash
> Might help the blind, not him, serenely sly.[46]

Fortunately for the life of his art if not for the tidiness of his thought, Stevens' practice proved incapable of adhering to his principle. As the poems of *Ideas of Order* would prove a decade later, Stevens' renunciation of euphuism would be no more final than his rejection of the symbolic south. He would remain the master of two styles, and the uneasy lover of two worlds—the one that is and the one that might come to be.

Notes

NOTES TO CHAPTER I

1. "A Postcard from the Volcano," *The Collected Poems of Wallace Stevens* (New York, 1957), pp. 158–59. Hereafter I will refer to this volume as *CP*.
2. Cf. Mildred E. Hartstock, "Stevens' 'Bantams in Pine Woods,'" *The Explicator*, XVIII (March 1960), 33. Miss Harstock's imaginative thesis is that in this poem Stevens is concerned with "the poet's place in the evolutionary process itself of which the cock is the general symbol." In fairness to Miss Harstock, I should add that her explication does not precisely illustrate the fallacy I am discussing. It is doubtful, for instance, that merely by studying "what is there on the page" she could gloss the imprecation "Damned universal cock" by suggesting that "the cock (or the poet) is damned because the individual of any species is damned: that is, doomed to death and extinction no matter how creative he may have been."
3. "The Mechanical Optimist," first published separately in *New Directions in Prose and Poetry*, ed. James Laughlin (1936), appeared a year later in *The Man with the Blue Guitar and Other Poems* as the first stanza of "A Thought Revolved."

4. "Wallace Stevens, or The Hedonist's Progress," *In Defense of Reason* (New York, 1943), pp. 445–46.
5. *Poems by Wallace Stevens,* ed. Samuel French Morse, (New York, 1959), p. vii.
6. *Ibid.,* p. viii. Despite Stevens' occasional expressions of dissatisfaction with *Harmonium,* he seems never seriously to have doubted the volume's central importance to his total achievement. This is evidenced not only by his continual fascination with the book's title, but also by the fact that when in the early fifties Stevens selected poems to be included in the Faber and Faber *Selected Poems,* thirty-four of the fifty-eight he chose were from *Harmonium.*
7. Quoted by Samuel French Morse, "The Native Element," *Kenyon Review,* XX (Summer 1958), 452.
8. "Wallace Stevens: The World as Meditation," *Literature and Belief, English Institute Essays, 1957* (New York, 1958), p. 151. The quotations from Stevens may be found on pp. 58 and 61 of *The Necessary Angel* (New York, 1951).
9. *Opus Posthumous,* ed. Samuel French Morse (New York, 1957); the first two aphorisms appear on p. 162, the third on p. 164, the fourth and fifth on p. 166, the sixth on p. 168, and the last on p. 175. Hereafter I will refer to this volume as *OP.*
10. *CP,* p. 215.
11. "The Figure of the Youth as Virile Poet," *The Necessary Angel* (New York, 1951). Hereafter I will refer to this volume as *NA.*
12. "Well Moused, Lion," *Dial,* LXXVI (January 1924), 91. The phrase is originally Stevens'; in "The Comedian as the Letter C" (*CP,* p. 31), we are told of Crispin: "His violence was for aggrandizement/ And not for stupor."
13. *Ibid.,* p. 84.
14. "Public Verse" [Review of William Stanley Braithewaite's *Anthology for Magazine Verse for 1915],* New Republic, VI (March 25, 1916), 223.
15. Letter in "The Reader Critic," *The Little Review,* V (July 1918), 61.

16. "The Revival of Aestheticism," *The Freeman,* VIII (December 19, 1923), 355.
17. *Ibid.*
18. *Ibid.,* p. 356.
19. "The Thirteenth Way," *Dial,* LXXVII (July 1924), 47.
20. *Ibid.,* p. 45.
21. "Of Modern Poetry," *CP,* p. 239.
22. "The Dandyism of Wallace Stevens," *Dial,* LXXIX (November 1925), 416.
23. *Ibid.,* p. 414.
24. Fletcher, "The Revival of Aestheticism," p. 356.
25. "The Noble Rider and the Sound of Words," *NA,* pp. 30–31.
26. *Ibid.,* p. 30.
27. *Ibid.,* p. 26.
28. "The Words of the World," *Encounter,* XIV (April 1960), 45.
29. "Three Academic Pieces," *NA,* p. 81.
30. "Examples of Wallace Stevens," *Language as Gesture* (New York, 1952), pp. 221–22.
31. *Ibid.,* p. 226. For Stevens' own justification of euphuism ("a reason in the sun for metaphor") see "Three Academic Pieces," *NA,* p. 78.
32. "Turmoil in the Middle Ground," *New Masses,* XVII (October 1, 1935), 42. Stevens responded to the Burnshaw review by entitling a section of his long poem "Owl's Clover," "Mr. Burnshaw and the Statue." And in a letter to Ronald Lane Latimer dated October 9, 1935 (The Ronald Lane Latimer Papers, University of Chicago Library), he remarked that the Burnshaw review was "most interesting"

> "because it placed me in a new setting. I hope I am headed left, but there are lefts and lefts, and certainly I am not headed for the ghastly left of MASSES. The rich man and the comfortable man of the imagination of people like Mr. Burnshaw are not nearly so rich nor nearly so comfortable as he believes them to be. And, what is more, his poor men

are not nearly so poor. These professionals lament in a way that would have given Job a fever."

Later in the same letter, however, Stevens added: "I do very much believe in leftism in every direction, even in wailing. . . . [The leftists] have the most magnificent cause in the world."

A remark of Mr. Burnshaw's in a letter to me provides an amusing postscript to the rather complex affair: "I am grateful for your explication of the poem ["Owl's Clover"]. It holds together for me—and then I begin to wonder why one should have to work so on what is rather an indifferent piece of creative work. You see, I don't think I've been immortalized by Stevens, really; the poem in which I figure is not, alas, as good as I should have wished it to be."

33. "Turmoil in the Middle Ground," p. 42.

34. "Connoisseur of Chaos," *CP*, p. 215.

35. "The Vicissitudes of Reputation, 1914–1940," *Harvard Advocate*, CXXVII (December 1940), 40.

36. *Ibid.*, p. 44.

37. *Ibid.*, p. 32.

38. *Ibid.*, p. 23.

39. *Ibid.*

40. *Ibid.*, p. 25.

41. *Ibid.*, p. 31.

42. "A Foreword," *In Defense of Reason*, p. 11.

43. *Ibid.*, p. 13.

44. It is true that pp. 449–56 of "Wallace Stevens, or The Hedonist's Progress" (*In Defense of Reason*) trace the history of the romantic tradition from which, in Winters' view, Stevens' hedonism springs. The discussion, however, consists largely of a diatribe against eighteenth-century deism and rationalism, against the vague melancholy of early romanticism, and against the symbolic techniques first suggested by Coleridge in his doctrine of organic form, then communicated, through Poe, to the French symbolists, from whom Stevens learned them.

45. Winters, "A Foreword," p. 5.

46. Winters, "Wallace Stevens, or The Hedonist
    p. 433.
47. *Ibid.*, pp. 433–34.
48. *Ibid.*, p. 437.
49. *Ibid.*, p. 439.
50. "Wallace Stevens: The World as Meditation,"
    and Belief, p. 143.
51. "The Poetry of Wallace Stevens," *Poetry,* LXXV (December 1949), 151.
52. *Ibid.*, p. 152.
53. *Ibid.*
54. "Reflections on Wallace Stevens," *Poetry and the Age* (New York, 1953), p. 139.
55. *Ibid.*, p. 140.
56. "Absence in Reality: A Study of the Epistemology of the Blue Guitar," *Kenyon Review,* XXI (Fall 1959), 547.
57. "The Realistic Oriole: A Study of Wallace Stevens," *Hudson Review,* X (Autumn 1957), 353.
58. "Absence in Reality," p. 547. Cf. Frank Doggett, "Wallace Stevens' Later Poetry" *ELH,* XXV (June 1958), 153: "Stevens, in spite of appearance is never a philosophical poet except (like other poets) in his interest in the theory of reality. One can answer some attempts to distill a system of ideas from his poetry by another and divergent distillation. His ideas are not systematic but thematic. What seems a development of doctrine is a version of experience."
59. "An Ordinary Evening in New Haven," *CP,* pp. 488–89.
60. "A Collect of Philosophy," *OP,* p. 191.
61. "Wallace Stevens' Later Poetry," *ELH,* XXV (June 1958), 150.
62. Robert Pack, in the conclusion to his recent study, *Wallace Stevens: An Approach to his Poetry and Thought* (New Brunswick, New Jersey, 1958), pp. 197–98, places renewed and sympathetic emphasis on Stevens' hedonism when he writes: "The luxury of this comfort and this well-being is that it allows men to explore the range of their thoughts, to experience the variety of sensuous pleasures, and with this luxury Stevens achieves his success and con-

ceives of an earthly paradise in some of the most witty, profound and beautiful poems in the English language."

Pack's cogent explanation of Stevens' hedonism may profitably be compared with Mill's familiar tribute to Wordsworth, whose poems "expressed, not mere outward beauty, but states of feeling and of thought colored by feeling, under the excitement of beauty. They seemed to be the very culture of feelings, which I was in quest of. In them I seemed to draw from a source of inward joy, of sympathetic and imaginative pleasure, which could be shared in by all human beings; which has no connection with struggle or imperfection, but would be made richer by every improvement in the physical or social condition of mankind. From them I seemed to learn what would be the perennial source of happiness, when all the greater evils of life should have been removed."

63. "The Genre of Wallace Stevens," *Sewanee Review*, XIII (October 1945), 566.
64. "The Humanism of Wallace Stevens," *Poetry*, LXI (November 1942), 451.
65. "The Genre of Wallace Stevens," pp. 572–73.
66. "The World of Wallace Stevens," *Modern American Poetry: Focus Five*, ed. B. Rajan (London, 1950), pp. 105, 109.
67. "The Poetry of Wallace Stevens," *Partisan Review*, XVI (September 1949), 909.
68. *Ibid.*, 895.
69. See notes 56 and 57 of this chapter for reference to the Stallknecht and Frye essays.
70. Wallace Stevens: The Life of the Imagination," *PMLA*, LXVI (September 1951), 572.
71. *Wallace Stevens: An Approach to His Poetry and Thought* (New Brunswick, New Jersey, 1958), p. 196. Cf. n. 62 of this chapter for an exception to my general indictment of Pack.
72. Three more recent comprehensive but short studies of Stevens' *oeuvre* deserve mention. The shortest of these, William York Tindall's essay in the University of Minne-

sota Pamphlets on American Writers series (*Wallace Stevens*, Minneapolis, 1961) is by all standards the slightest. Mr. Tindall, both in his general remarks and in his practical criticism, is inclined to restrict himself to the fringes of Stevens' thought and art, and his strenuous contempt for any organizing principle prevents him from marshaling his occasionally keen insights into a coherent view. Frank Kermode's long essay (*Wallace Stevens*, Edinburgh and London, 1961) is one of the best general introductions to Stevens now available, and contains admirable readings of individual poems. Roy Harvey Pearce's essay on "Wallace Stevens and the Ultimate Poem" in *The Continuity of American Poetry* (Princeton, 1961), pp. 376–419, is an excellent study of Stevens' mode of affirmation—despite some surprising lapses. (Cf. Pearce's discussion of sun and the creative seasons on p. 379; his unconvincing reading of "Thirteen Ways of Looking at a Blackbird" on pp. 382–83; and his failure [pp. 389–90] to consider *Ideas of Order* against the social context in which its poems were written.) In the past decade, several invaluable checklists of Stevens' writing and of criticism of his work have appeared. Principal among these: Samuel French Morse, *Wallace Stevens, A Preliminary Checklist of His Published Writings: 1898–1954* (New Haven, 1954); Ashley Brown and Robert S. Haller, *The Achievement of Wallace Stevens* (Philadelphia, 1962), pp. 271–87; Jackson R. Bryer and Joseph N. Riddel, "A Checklist of Stevens Criticism," *Twentieth Century Literature*, VIII, Nos. 3–4 (October 1962–January 1963), 124–42; and Roger S. Mitchell, "Wallace Stevens: A Checklist of Criticism," *Bulletin of Bibliography*, Vol. 23, Nos. 9–10 (September–December 1962, January–April 1963) 208–11, 232–33.

73. CP, pp. 158–59. The ellipsis is Stevens'. In an undergraduate sonnet—"Vita Mea," *Harvard Advocate*, LXVI (December 12, 1893), 78—there are foreshadowings of the shuttered mansion and storming spirit images of "A Postcard from the Volcano." The octet, with which the parallels end, follows:

With fear I trembled in the House of Life,
Hast'ning from door to door, from room to room,
Seeking a way from that impenetrable gloom
Against whose walls my strength lay weak from strife.
All dark! All dark! And what sweet wind was rife
With earth, or sea, or star, or new sun's bloom,
Lay sick and dead within that place of doom,
Where I went raving like the winter's wife.

74. William Butler Yeats, "Lapis Lazuli," *Collected Poems* (New York, 1952)), p. 292.

NOTES TO CHAPTER II

1. Quoted by Michael Lafferty, "Wallace Stevens: A Man of Two Worlds," *Historical Review of Berks County*, XXIV (Fall 1959), 131. Although the quotation is unquestionably vintage Stevens, it presents a minor problem in verification. Lafferty cites his source as a *Time* interview of 1955; but although *Time* does quote Stevens in an obituary notice of August 15 (LXVI, 12), only the first and fourth sentences of the remarks quoted by Lafferty appear there. No other stories on Stevens appeared in *Time* in 1955.

2. *The Shaping Spirit: A Study of Wallace Stevens* (Chicago, 1950), p. 4.

3. "As You Leave the Room," *OP*, p. 117.

4. "Adagia," *OP*, p. 167.

5. Quoted by Lafferty, *op. cit.*, p. 110. On the question of Stevens' political affiliation, it is interesting to compare William York Tindall's statement that "Stevens was a Republican, a Taft Republican, who thought Eisenhower a dangerous radical," *Wallace Stevens*, University of Minnesota Pamphlets on American Writers (Minneapolis, 1961), p. 9. Stevens' own statement and Tindall's are not, of course, irreconcilable. A letter from Miss Holly Stevens to me suggests that Stevens' attachment to the Democratic party lapsed during the course of Roosevelt's first term.

6. Lafferty, p. 110.

7. *Ibid.*
8. *Ibid.*, p. 113. Lafferty states that Stevens met his future wife while he was still an undergraduate at Harvard, but in fact they met in the summer of 1904 when he returned to Reading after passing his bar exams.
9. *Ibid.*, p. 110.
10. *Ibid.*, p. 111. Although I have followed Lafferty's assumption that Stevens intended all along to be a lawyer, there appears to be evidence in Stevens' journal and in his letters to his father from 1897–1908 that he turned to law only after failing at journalism. These materials are not, at the moment I write, available for study.
11. "Verlaine in Hartford: Has the Mystery Man of Modern Poetry Really Another Self?" *View*, I (September 1940), 6.
12. *Ibid.*
13. *Ibid.* For a detailed study of Stevens' undergraduate verse, see Robert Buttell, "Wallace Stevens at Harvard: Some Origins of his Theme and Style," *ELH*, XXIX (March 1962), 90–119. My own discussion owes nothing to Buttell's.
14. "The Irrational Element in Poetry," *OP*, p. 218.
15. "Adagia," *OP*, p. 177.
16. *Harvard Advocate*, LXVII (April 10, 1899), 18.
17. *Ibid.*, LXVIII (November 13, 1899), 104.
18. *Ibid.*
19. *Ibid.*, LXIX (April 13, 1900), 50.
20. *Ibid.* LXVII (April 10, 1899), 18. The last line of the poem echoes Wordsworth's sonnet "Composed upon Westminster Bridge."
21. *CP*, p. 18.
22. *Harvard Advocate*, LXVII (April 10, 1899), 18.
23. Randall Jarrell, *Poetry and the Age* (New York, 1953), p. 134.
24. Letter dated September 23, 1922, in Wallace Stevens Manuscripts, Harriet Monroe Modern Poetry Library, University of Chicago.
25. *Pleasure Dome* (Boston and Cambridge, 1949), p. 197.

26. Cf. R. P. Blackmur, *Language as Gesture* (New York, 1952), p. 221.
27. "Three Academic Pieces," *NA*, p. 78.
28. "The Noble Rider and the Sound of Words," *NA*, p. 35.
29. *Ibid.*, p. 36.
30. Quoted by Samuel French Morse, ed. *OP*, p. xvii.
31. *Ibid.*
32. I here follow the chronology of Michael Lafferty, "Wallace Stevens: A Man of Two Worlds," p. 112, which would appear to be more accurate than that of O'Connor, who, on p. 14 of *The Shaping Spirit*, places Stevens' experience with the *New York Tribune* after his graduation from law school.
33. Quoted by O'Connor, pp. 14–15. One of the newspaper offices in which Stevens' story has apparently *not* become famous is that of the New York *Herald Tribune*. In reply to a query from me, Mr. Robert E. Grayson, director of the *Herald Tribune's* editorial library, writes that he could locate no mention of the "flotsam" story, nor indeed was he able to find any record of Stevens' brief career with the *Tribune* save for the statement in the *Herald Tribune's* own obituary on Stevens that he had been a reporter for that paper.
34. Lafferty, p. 113. A letter to me from Miss Holly Stevens suggests that 1903 is a somewhat early date to mark the beginning of Stevens' climb to material success. In the five years that followed his graduation from law school, he changed law firms several times and was frequently broke, until, in 1908, he joined an insurance company (The American Bonding Company).
35. Quoted by Hi Simons, "Vicissitudes of Reputation, 1914–1940," *Harvard Advocate*, CXXVII (December 1940), 8.
36. Wallace Stevens Manuscripts, Harriet Monroe Modern Poetry Library, University of Chicago.
37. *OP*, pp. 4–5. Among noncombatant poets writing at this time, Stevens was not alone in seeing war as a means of transcending the vulgar and aimless workaday present;

cf., for instance, Yeats's much richer but not dissimilar poem, "An Irish Airman Foresees His Death."

38. Wallace Stevens Manuscripts.
39. *Ibid.*; cf. *OP*, p. xviii.
40. *The Letters of D. H. Lawrence* (N. Y., 1932), p. 215.
41. Ford, "Verlaine in Hartford," p. 6.
42. *Business Week* (April 8, 1950), p. 9.
43. *The Way It Was* (New York, 1959), pp. 12–13.
44. *A History of American Poetry: Our Singing Strength* (2d ed.; New York, 1934), pp. 502–3.
45. *Ibid.*, p. 500. A letter I received from Mr. Van Vechten casts some new light on the circumstances behind the publication of *Harmonium*; I quote it in full: "I certainly did not 'cajole' Alfred Knopf into publishing Harmonica [sic], but I did submit it to him with enthusiasm and he accepted it with pleasure, already being somewhat familiar with Wallace Stevens' poems. I do not recall "indifference' on the part of WS. Some years later, Mr. Knopf gave a luncheon for Stevens, at which I was present, on the occasion of his eightieth birthday [Stevens in fact died in his seventy-fifth year]. Wallace made a speech in which he said approximately that I had been responsible for his initial publication with a publisher with whom he had remained ever since: Harmonica. I was not sitting at Stevens' table, and as I am very deaf, I did not understand a word of this, but Irita Van Doren, on my right, repeated it to me verbatim, a little too late for me to voice my thanks. The 'dying magazine of parts' was called The Trend and I think Wallace's two poems which appeared herein were the first he had published, but in this I may be in error." (Mr. Van Vechten had referred in his "Notes for an Autobiography" to Stevens only as a contributor to "a dying magazine of parts." Although Samuel French Morse's original *Checklist* omits mention of Stevens' early contributions to *The Trend,* the recent revision of the *Checklist* confirms the late Mr. Van Vechten's recollection. Stevens published eight poems in the September 1914 number of *The Trend* and two in the

November number; Samuel French Morse *et al.*, *Wallace Stevens Checklist and Bibliography of Stevens Criticism* (Denver, 1963), p. 52.

46. William Carlos Williams, *Kora in Hell* (Boston, 1920), p. 18.

    In 1960 I wrote to Mr. Conrad Aiken asking for his view of my general thesis that, briefly stated, Stevens was uncertain, particularly in the years before his poetic reputation was secure, how seriously to take his own poetry, and that this uncertainty had effects observable both in his literary career and in the poetry itself. I quote from Mr. Aiken's reply:

    Thanks for your letter, and very interesting that idea is—true too, I think, and I think too that in a submerged sort of way I have always been aware of it. And perhaps I *can* adduce a shadow of evidence that it was something Stevens was *himself* aware of. In 1933 or 1934 I suggested to J. M. Dent, via Richard Church, that they should bring out HARMONIUM in their poetry series, and I was asked to write Stevens about this, or rather, to ask him for a new book—in their perverse way, they didn't want a book ten years old. Stevens in due course replied that he didn't have anything, he hadn't been writing. End of correspondence. In 1936 I first met him at Ted Spencer's, after he had given a reading in Sanders Theatre. When we were introduced, he at once said that he regarded me as the godfather of all his recent work, and that it was my request for a book for Dent that had started him off again. This would certainly fit in with your theory that he hadn't himself known how seriously to take himself, that the comparative failure of HARMONIUM abetted his self-doubts, and that perhaps along with this went a graver doubt as to the value of the poet and poetry, especially in U S society of that period. . . . Of course, a further element in all this was the fact that the members of the OTHERS group—Williams, Bodenheim, Kreymborg, Djuna Barnes, Mina Loy, et al, by their constant reference to him as a 'dandy,' may have contributed to this feeling that he was not quite *in it* but somewhere to one side, and with a difference—not engaged or dedicated in the same way. And then, of course, with returning confidence, nothing would have been more natural (it was already implicit in MONOCLE) than that he should construct a theory which would justify the whole corpus, even to the extremes of ironic or humorous self-disparagement.

47. *A History of American Poetry*, p. 500.
48. Quoted by O'Connor. *The Shaping Spirit*, p. 15.
49. *Troubadour: An Autobiography* (New York, 1925), p. 332.
50. *Ibid.* p. 239.
51. *Ibid.* p. 220.
52. *Men Seen* (New York, 1925), p. 159.
53. *A Critical Fable* (Boston and New York, 1924), p. 97.
54. "A Talk with Mr. Stevens," *The New York Times Book Review* (October 3, 1954), p. 3.
55. Only two of the plays have been published. *Three Travelers Watch a Sunrise,* which first appeared in *Poetry,* VIII (July 1916), 163–79 and was the winner of a prize sponsored by the Player's Producing Company, and *Carlos Among the Candles,* which appeared in *Poetry,* XI (December 1917), 115–23, have been collected by Samuel French Morse, ed., *OP.* The third play, *Bowl, Cat and Broomstick,* remains in manuscript. (Cf. *OP,* pp. xxvi–xxxi.)
56. "Red Loves Kit," *OP,* p. 30.
57. Cf. Morse, ed., *OP,* p. xxxiii.
58. *CP,* p. 118.
59. Mr. Morse's phrase appears in a letter to me dated November 3, 1959.
60. *CP,* p. 41.
61. Wallace Stevens Manuscripts; letter originally undated but marked "1924" by Miss Monroe. As late as 1935 Stevens would still allude to the commercial failure of *Harmonium* with pungent wit, and a touch of bitterness. Thus, when Ronald Lane Latimer asked Stevens to inscribe his copy

of the book, Stevens wrote back: "I shall be happy to inscribe *Harmonium*. Some time ago a most agreeable damsel
called me up on the telephone to say that she was passing
through Hartford and would I inscribe her copy of *Harmonium*. I told her that I wondered that she did not
prefer to leave it without inscription, since, so far as I
know, that was the only copy without inscription in existence. But I find that I was, after all, mistaken.

"Now wouldn't it be much better just to paste this
amusing anecdote in your copy?" (The Ronald Lane Latimer Papers, University of Chicago Library, letter dated
January 8, 1935.)

62. Wallace Stevens Manuscripts, letter dated September 23,
1922.

63. *Ibid.,* letter dated October 28, 1922.

64. Louis Untermeyer Collection, Lilly Library, Indiana University: letter dated January 13, 1925.

65. Wallace Stevens Manuscripts, letter dated January 12,
1925.

66. Untermeyer Collection, letter dated March 3, 1925.

67. *Ibid.,* letter dated November 8, 1926.

68. Wallace Stevens Manuscripts, letter dated August 5, 1932.

69. "The Revival of Aestheticism," *The Freeman,* VIII (December 19, 1923), 355.

70. "The Noble Rider and the Sound of Words," *NA,* p. 30.

71. Wallace Stevens Manuscripts, letter dated September 23,
1922.

72. *Ibid.,* letter dated March 13, 1935.

73. *Ibid.,* letter dated April 5, 1935.

74. *Poetry and the Age,* p. 135.

75. *Leisure the Basis of Culture,* trans. Alexander Dru, with
an introduction by T. S. Eliot (London, 1952), p. 20.

76. For the "mickey mockers," see "The American Sublime,"
CP, p. 130.

77. *American Writing in the Twentieth Century* (Cambridge,
Mass., 1960) p. 227.

78. *The Four Ages of Poetry, etc.,* ed. H. F. B. Brett-Smith
(Oxford, 1952), pp. 16–17.

79. *CP*, p. 312.
80. "The Noble Rider and the Sound of Words," *NA*, p. 27.
81. "Like Decorations in a Nigger Cemetery," *CP*, p. 153.
82. "The Man with the Blue Guitar," *CP*, p. 180.
83. "Like Decorations in a Nigger Cemetery," *CP*, p. 154.
84. *Ibid.*, p. 155.
85. "Academic Discourse at Havana," *CP*, p. 144.

NOTES TO CHAPTER III

1. *The Invisible Poet* (New York, 1959), p. 17.
2. "Pure and Impure Poetry," *Selected Essays* (New York, 1958), p. 4.
3. *CP*, p. 53.
4. We have already seen evidence of this strain in Stevens' reluctance to publish and in his expressed distaste for the poems of *Harmonium*. More dramatic evidence of his lack of confidence in his own art appears in a letter dated June 6, 1915, to Harriet Monroe (Wallace Stevens Manuscripts, University of Chicago), in which he grants Miss Monroe permission to cut the eight-stanza version of "Sunday Morning" which later appeared in *Harmonium* to the five-stanza version published in *Poetry*. It has hitherto been supposed that Stevens expanded the poem after its original appearance in *Poetry*. In a letter dated June 23, 1915 (Wallace Stevens Manuscripts), Stevens asked Miss Monroe to suggest an emendation for two lines which she found difficult in the original version of "Sunday Morning." "I ask this," he remarked, "because your criticism is clearly well-founded." It is true that William Carlos Williams was also, on occasion, willing to abide by Miss Monroe's editorial suggestions; yet, even when he accepted them, he protested violently against changes far less drastic than those which Miss Monroe wrought on "Sunday Morning." (Cf. *The Selected Letters of William Carlos Williams* [New York, 1957], pp. 23–26.) On the other hand, when Miss Monroe proposed to shorten a piece by D. H. Lawrence, he replied: "Why, oh why,

do you want to cut off the tail of poor *Ophelia's* ballad?
... No, you musn't cut it in two. It is a good poem: I
couldn't do it again to save my life. Use it whole or not
at all. I return you the MS. If you don't use it, please
destroy it." Miss Monroe used it. (Cf. *The Letters of D.
H. Lawrence* [New York, 1932], pp. 210–12.)

5. *OP,* p. 20.

6. "The Florist Wears Knee-Breeches," which does not appear
in *OP,* may be found in *Others,* II (March 1916), 173,
or in *Others: An Anthology of the New Verse,* ed. Alfred
Kreymborg (New York, 1916), p. 128. The title suggests
that the poet lives in the past.

7. *OP,* p. 25.

8. "Peter Parasol" develops, with ineffectual irony, the theme
of its opening quatrain:

> *Why are not women fair,*
> *All, as Andromache,*
> *Having, each one, most praisable*
> *Ears, eyes, souls, skins, hair?*

In a letter dated August 16, 1919 (Wallace Stevens Manuscripts), Stevens anticipated my criticism by urging Miss
Monroe not to print the poem; his reasons were "that the
element of pastiche . . . will not be apparent and the poem
will go off on its substance and not on its style. . . ."
"Peter Parasol" was published nevertheless in the October
1919 number of *Poetry.*

   "The Florist Wears Knee-Breeches," although it aspires higher than "Peter Parasol" and provides hints of
one of Stevens' favorite themes—the reciprocal influence
between man and the natural objects which surround
him—is essentially a sentimental love lyric.

9. "The Comedian as the Letter C," *CP,* pp. 27–46; "Peter
Quince at the Clavier," *CP,* pp. 89–92. Stevens' figure of the
poet-clown, particularly in "The Comedian," has parallels
in the Pierrot of Laforgue and in Valéry's modern "Euro-
pean Hamlet," who

> stares at millions of ghosts. But he is an intellectual Ham-
> let. He meditates on the life and death of truths. For

phantoms he has all the subjects of our controversies; for regrets, he has all our titles to glory; he bows under the weight of discoveries and learning, unable to renounce and unable to resume this limitless activity. He reflects on the boredom of recommencing the past, on the folly of always striving to be original. He wavers between one abyss and the other, for two dangers still threaten the world: order and disorder. (Quoted by Warren Ramsey, *Jules Laforgue and the Ironic Inheritance* [New York, 1953], p. 133.) For a valuable discussion of the clown as a stage in the development of Stevens' poetic hero see Michel Benamou, "Le Thème du Héros dans la Poésie de Wallace Stevens," *Études anglaises*, XII (1959), 107–17.

10. The nude herself, who is a figure of the muse as well as of the sunrise, takes on ironic coloring through her paltriness.

11. This same subject, handled less obliquely, becomes the theme of "Bantams in Pine-Woods."

12. Walter W. Skeat, *An Etymological Dictionary of the English Language* (Oxford, 1882), p. 24.

13. *Poetry*, XIX (October 1921), 1–9.

14. *Pleasure Dome* (Boston and Cambridge, 1949), p. 198. To the best of my knowledge, Stevens was never an insurance salesman.

15. "Wallace Stevens and E. E. Cummings," *The Shores of Light* (London, 1952), p. 50.

16. *Axel's Castle* (New York, 1931), pp. 292–93.

17. "Farewell to Florida," *CP*, p. 118.

18. Cf. Norman Brown, *Life Against Death* (New York, 1959), p. 56. In "The Noble Rider and the Sound of Words" (*NA*, pp. 14–15) Stevens summarizes but does not directly come to terms with the argument Freud advances in *The Future of an Illusion* that man must eventually surrender to reality, however cruel he may find that reality to be. A more direct attempt by Stevens to reconcile Freud's ideas with his own may be found in "Imagination as Value," *NA*, pp. 139 ff.

Stevens' view of realism is suggested by the adage, "Realism is a corruption of reality" ("Adagia," *OP*, p. 166).

19. See for example, "The Noble Rider and the Sound of Words," *NA*, p. 17; "The Imagination as Value," *NA*, pp. 136–39; "Adagia," *OP*, pp. 160, 163, 169, 171–72, 180; "Two or Three Ideas," *OP*, p. 215, "Williams," *OP*, p. 256.

20. Quoted by Stevens, "Imagination as Value," *NA*, p. 136.

21. *Time and Western Man* (Boston, 1957; 1st ed. 1927), p. 6.

22. "Two or Three Ideas," *OP*, p. 215.

23. This concept of reality as including more than the empirical present is implicit in the adage quoted in n. 18 of this chapter and explicit in the following one: "Reality is not what it is. It consists of the many realities which it can be made into" ("Adagia," *OP*, p. 178).

24. "Two or Three Ideas," *OP*, p. 215.

25. For Stevens' views on the violence of contemporary reality, see "The Noble Rider and the Sound of Words," *NA*, *passim*. For his view on the inadequacy of private aesthetic experience, see the following adage: "Religion is dependent on faith. But aesthetics is independent of faith. The relative positions of the two might be reversed. It is possible to establish aesthetics in the individual mind as immeasurably a greater thing than religion. Its present state is the result of the difficulty of establishing it except in the individual mind." ("Adagia," *OP*, p. 166).

26. *The letters of John Keats*, ed. Maurice Buston Forman (London, 1935), p. 68.

27. *Life Against Death* (New York, 1959), p. 60.

28. *Ibid.*, p. 57.

29. *Ibid.*

30. "Imagination as Value," *NA*, p. 138.

31. *Ibid.*

32. *Ibid.*, p. 139.

33. See especially: "A dead romantic is a falsification" ("Adagia," *OP*, p. 160); and: "It should be said of poetry that it is essentially romantic as if one were recognizing the truth about poetry for the first time. Although the

romantic is referred to, most often, in a pejorative sense, this sense attaches, or should attach, not to the romantic in general but to some phase of the romantic that has become stale. Just as there is always a romantic that is potent, there is always a romantic that is impotent" ("Adagia," *OP,* p. 180). See also *OP,* pp. 215–16 and 254–57.

34. Freud offers what may be a more meaningful explanation of the general problem of poetic irony in the passage on "wit" that follows. Norman Brown, commenting on the passage, suggests "that the word 'art' can be substituted for the word 'wit.' "

> [Wit] begins as play, in order to derive pleasure from the free use of words and ideas. As soon as the strengthening reason forbids this play with words as senseless and with ideas as foolish, it turns to the joke in order to retain these sources of pleasure and to be able to gain new pleasures from the liberation of the nonsensical. As real but non-tendentious wit it assists ideas and strengthens them against the assault of critical judgment, utilizing in this process the principle of interchange of pleasure sources; and finally it joins with the major tendencies struggling against repression, in order to remove inner inhibitions according to the principle of fore-pleasure.

(Quoted by Brown, *Life Against Death,* p. 64.) There are numerous examples of this kind of process in Stevens' poetry; see, for example, "Snow and Stars," *CP,* 133.

35. The three quotations are from "Adagia," *OP,* p. 178.

36. *Ibid.,* p. 168.

37. "The Noble Rider and the Sound of Words," *NA, passim.* The text reads "follow their readers," but this is an obvious misprint.

38. *Ibid.,* p. 29.

39. Cf. n. 25 of this chapter and see the following adages: "After one has abandoned a belief in god [sic], poetry is that essence which takes its place in life's redemption"; and "The relation of art to life is of the first importance, especially in a skeptical age since, in the absence of a

belief in God, the mind turns to its own creations and examines them, not alone from the aesthetic point of view, but for what they reveal, for what they validate and invalidate, for the support that they give" ("Adagia," *OP*, pp. 158–59).

40. "The Noble Rider and the Sound of Words," *NA*, p. 31. Cf. Norman Brown's summary of Freud's theory of art: "the conception of art derived from what Freud says about wit is substantial enough to constitute a psychoanalytical theory of art. Art as pleasure, art as play, art as a mode of instinctual liberation" (*Life Against Death*, pp. 65–66).

41. "Adagia," *OP*, p. 157.

42. "Life is Motion," *CP*, p. 83.

43. "Adagia," *OP*, p. 165.

44. See, for example, "Notes Toward a Supreme Fiction," *CP*, p. 401.

45. *CP*, pp. 89–92.

46. *CP*, p. 12. This delicate lyric begins with an analogy between the motion of a glade-boat and the motion of the water through which it goes. That pattern of motion, which is the poem's true subject, is then further defined in terms of implied or stated analogies between the water and the green saw-grass through which *it* flows, between rainbows and "bedizened birds," between the whistling of the wind and the whistling of kildeer; until at the close of the poem we return to its beginning, or to the fringes of its beginning; the metaphoric whistling birds become "real" as "they rise/ At the red turban/ Of the boatman." It is impossible in a brief analysis even fully to suggest the complex patterns of resemblance Stevens establishes. The end result of this particular lyric pattern is that each image contains all of the images, and the reader experiences a startling synthesis of motion and stasis.

47. See Brown, *Life Against Death*, p. 41. Brown's chapter on "The Self and the Other: Narcissus," in which this reference occurs, is of great interest in suggesting a psychosexual basis for aesthetics.

48. "Adagia," *OP*, p. 163.

49. "The Comedian as the Letter C," *CP*, p. 35.

NOTES TO CHAPTER IV

1. "Another way of Looking at the Blackbird," *New Republic,* CXXXVII (November 4, 1957), 17.

2. On p. 162 of his essay on "The Poetry of Wallace Stevens," *Poetry,* LXXV (December 1949), 149–65, J. V. Cunningham cites passages from the poem he refers to as *The Recluse* which bear out his claim that the rhetoric and "the positive argument" of "Sunday Morning" owe something to the influence of Wordsworth.

   In 1953, Renato Poggioli, who was then engaged in translating Stevens into Italian, apparently queried Stevens on this point. I have not seen Poggioli's letter, but in his reply dated June 3, 1953, Stevens wrote: "I don't remember *The Recluse* and could not find it offhand." (Wallace Stevens Manuscripts, Houghton Library, Harvard University.) According to Holly Stevens, however, her father seems to have been referring to an unidentified poem of his own.

3. "The Irrational Element in Poetry," *OP,* p. 222. The Plato reference appears specifically to allude to *Republic* VI. 508.

4. "Imagination as Value," *NA,* p. 142.

5. "Le Monocle de Mon Oncle," *CP,* p. 17.

6. *OP,* p. 159.

7. "The Noble Rider and the Sound of Words," *NA,* p. 31.

8. "Adagia," *OP,* p. 163.

9. That she is female is in accord with the poem's feminine "Virgilian cadences" (cf. "Notes Toward a Supreme Fiction," *CP,* p. 407), and also with Stevens' practice, alluded to in the previous chapter, of identifying woman with the pleasure principle.

10. "Three Academic Pieces," *NA,* p. 77.

11. See Chapter III, note 46, for a brief discussion of a similar associative technique employed by Stevens in "The Load of Sugar Cane."

12. "The Comedian as the Letter C," *CP,* p. 31.

13. "Life is Motion," *CP,* p. 83.

14. In the essay "Two or Three Ideas," first published in 1951, Stevens' examination of the idea that "the gods of classical mythology were merely aesthetic projections, . . . not the objects of belief," provides a prose commentary on this stanza (*OP*, pp. 207–8).

15. James Boswell, *The Life of Dr. Johnson*, ed. R. W. Chapman (London, 1957), p. 240.

16. Wallace Stevens Manuscripts, Harriet Monroe Modern Poetry Library, University of Chicago; letter dated June 23, 1915.

17. A note dated September 23, 1915, from Stevens to Miss Monroe reads: "The lines seem perfectly all right to me in the proof and I am satisfied to have them go through in their present form. Thanks for your kindness in bearing the matter in mind." The revised version of "Sunday Morning" was published in the November number of *Poetry*.

19. Stevens constructs a similar network of images through his recurrent use of fruit as symbol of the bounty of the earth. The symbol occurs in five of the eight stanzas.

20. Randall Jarrell, "Reflections on Wallace Stevens," *Poetry and the Age* (New York, 1953), p. 139.

21. "The Figure of the Youth as Virile Poet," *NA*, p. 58.

22. "The Noble Rider and the Sound of Words," *NA*, p. 8.

23. "The Comedian as the Letter C," *CP*, p. 39.

24. Cf. "The Noble Rider and the Sound of Words," *NA*, p. 35, where Stevens remarks that "The nobility of rhetoric is, of course, a lifeless nobility."

NOTES TO CHAPTER V

1. There are numerous statements of this conviction in Stevens' work. For an example, see this adage: "The relation of art to life is of the first importance in a skeptical age since, in the absence of a belief in God, the mind turns to its own creations and examines them, not alone from the aesthetic point of view, but for what they reveal, for what they validate and invalidate, for the support that they give." ("Adagia," *OP*, p. 159.)

2. "Imagination as Value," *NA*, p. 139.
3. "Adagia," *OP*, p. 176.
4. "The Man Whose Pharynx Was Bad," *CP*, p. 96.
5. "Honors and Acts," *OP*, p. 244.
6. For possible modes of experience in an "unfallen" world, see Norman Brown's chapter on "Death, Time, and Eternity," *Life Against Death*, pp. 86–109.
7. The seeds of the argument I have been pursuing may be found in Stevens' essays "The Noble Rider and the Sound of Words" and "The Figure of the Youth as Virile Poet," *NA*, pp. 3–36 and pp. 39–67. Although my discussion is not a strict paraphrase, it sums up the spirit and some of the substance of these essays.
8. "Of Modern Poetry," *CP*, pp. 239–40.
9. "The Well Dressed Man with a Beard," "Extracts from Addresses to the Academy of Fine Ideas," *CP*, pp. 247, 257.
10. "Academic Discourse at Havana," *CP*, p. 143.
11. "Like Decorations in a Nigger Cemetery," *CP*, p. 157.
12. "Girl in a Nightgown," *CP*, p. 214.
13. *CP*, pp. 6–7.
14. *CP*, p. 68.
15. *OP*, p. 99.
16. *CP*, pp. 75–76.
17. *CP*, p. 92.
18. This theory and practice of poetry as expressive of the mind that makes it is of course original neither with Stevens nor with contemporary poets in general. H. M. Abrams' account of romantic expressive theories, and especially the theory of J. S. Mill, suggests the close parallels between Stevens' poetics and the general trend of Romantic poetical theory. (M. H. Abrams, *The Mirror and the Lamp* [New York, 1953], pp. 24–25.)

    As we shall see later in this chapter, to say that a poem is an act of the mind is for Stevens not essentially different from saying that *all* perception is primarily an act of the mind. The vision our eye records is no more "real" than the vision the poem records.
19. Letter dated October 28, 1922, Wallace Stevens Manu-

scripts, Harriet Monroe Modern Library, University of Chicago. Cf. Chapter II, note 64.

20. *CP*, pp. 53–54.

21. *CP*, p. 405.

22. Quoted by Norman Brown, *Life Against Death*, p. 92.

23. For examples of this idea in *Harmonium*, see "The Idea of a Colony" (fourth section of "The Comedian as the Letter C"), *CP*, pp. 36–40, and "Theory," *CP*, pp. 86–87. Stevens held this view in common with Blake, whose Prophetic Books have as a recurrent theme: "All who see become what they behold. . . ."

24. That in these lines Stevens is providing a statement of his own aesthetic aim during this period may not be entirely clear when one reads the poem in isolation. It becomes clear, however, when we compare the quoted lines with a passage from "The Comedian as the Letter C" (*CP*, p. 31) in which Crispin perceived

> *That coolness for his heat came suddenly,*
> *And only, in the fables that he scrawled*
> *With his own quill, in its indigenous dew,*
> *Of an aesthetic tough, diverse, untamed,*
> *Incredible to prudes, the mint of dirt,*
> *Green barbarism turning paradigm.*

The conflict between sterile civilization and fecund barbarism, the former associated with the north and reality, the latter with the south and the imagination, is a common theme in Stevens. It also occupies an important place in the work of Howard Nemerov, who is probably the most skilled of Stevens' admirers among contemporary poets.

25. *NA*, p. 146.

26. "A Poet That Matters," *OP*, p. 252; cf. *ibid.*, p. 251.

27. "Sailing After Lunch," *CP*, p. 120.

28. *CP*, p. 61.

29. *CP*, p. 102–3.

30. *CP*, p. 167.

31. "No Possum, No Sop, No Taters," *CP*, pp. 293–94. The fruit imagery in "Sunday Morning" provides another example of this type of symbol.

32. "Montrachet-le-Jardin," *CP*, pp. 260–64.
33. "The Noble Rider and the Sound of Words," *NA*, p. 31.
34. The term "serpent-kin" also appears in "The Comedian as the Letter C" (*CP*, p. 32), where it is associated with the too juicy opulence of the earth.
35. "Six Significant Landscapes," *CP*, p. 75.
36. "Adagia," *OP*, p. 163.
37. "The Noble Rider and the Sound of Words," *NA*, p. 31.
38. Quoted by Abrams, *The Mirror and the Lamp*, p. 35.
39. *Ibid.*, p. 65.
40. "The Noble Rider and the Sound of Words," *NA*, p. 7.
41. *CP*, p. 335.
42. Northrop Frye, "The Realistic Oriole: A Study of Wallace Stevens," *The Hudson Review* (Autumn 1957), 355; cf. "The Noble Rider and the Sound of Words," *NA*, p. 26.
43. "One writes poetry, then, in order to approach the good in what is harmonious and orderly," Stevens, "The Irrational Element in Poetry," *OP*, p. 222.
44. "Thirteen Ways of Looking at a Blackbird," *CP*, p. 93.
45. Cf. Frank Kermode, "The Artist in Isolation," *Romantic Image* (London, 1961), pp. 1–29.
46. Albert Camus, *Neither Victims Nor Executioners* (New York, 1960) p. 5. In one respect, at least, Stevens was more perceptive than Camus. Whereas Camus assumed that our severance from the future is primarily the result of the experiences of the Second World War, Stevens, in "The Noble Rider and the Sound of Words" (*NA*, p. 21), saw the war as "only part of a war-like whole." In short, for Stevens the war was a particularly violent symptom of a disease that had long been incubating. His view might profitably be compared with the prophetic visions of world cataclysm recorded by Yeats in "The Second Coming" or by Lawrence in *Women in Love*.
47. "Introduction" to Frank Kermode's *Puzzles and Epiphanies* (New York, 1962), p. ix.
48. *Ibid.*, p. x. Cf. Hayden Caruth's recent essay on "Poets without Prophecy," *The Nation*, CXCVI, no. 15 (Apr. 27, 1963), 354–57. Caruth makes a persuasive case that the

same kind of literary Eisenhowerism that afflicts our critics has been equally persuasive among current poets.

49. Cf. Frye, "The Romantic Oriole," pp. 354–56.

50. "Three Academic Pieces," *NA*, p. 83.

51. *CP*, p. 129. Cf. Blake, "The Ghost of Abel": "Nature has no Outline, but Imagination has./ Nature has no tune, but Imagination has. Nature has no Supernatural & dissolves:/ Imagination is Eternity."

52. The remarkable poem "The Snow Man" (*CP*, pp. 9–10) illustrates this point negatively. In it, the poet achieves the Coleridgean "One Life" at the cost of becoming as inhuman as the landscape he observes. Stevens' conviction of the subhumanity of nature explains why, in an unpublished letter to Renato Poggioli, July 4, 1953, he spoke of his "stubborn and constantly repeated rejection of the earth as mother" (Houghton Library, Harvard University). Although Stevens made the remark in connection with section XVI of "The Man With the Blue Guitar," it has general implications.

53. "Notes Toward a Supreme Fiction," *CP*, p. 383.

54. *CP*, p. 3.

55. Frye, p. 355.

56. "The Man with the Blue Guitar," *CP*, p. 165.

57. *CP*, p. 51.

58. *CP*, p. 68.

59. *CP*, p. 76.

60. Roy Harvey Pearce's suggestion, in *The Continuity of American Poetry* (Princeton, 1961), p. 381, that the jar is a mason jar of the type which, especially in the South, was "often filled with corn whiskey–i.e. moonshine," is appealing if not convincing.

61. *Ibid.*

62. Newspaper story quoted by Frank Kermode, *Romantic Image*, p. 3. Cf. the case of El Greco, "who, according to anecdote, refused to leave a darkened room because 'the daylight disturbed his inner light.'" (M. H. Abrams, *The Mirror and the Lamp*, p. 43.)

63. *CP,* pp. 92–95.
64. Roy Harvey Pearce, *The Continuity of American Poetry,* p. 383.
65. In a letter to Renato Poggioli dated July 1, 1953, Stevens remarked: "The thin men of Haddam are entirely fictitious although some years ago one of the citizens of that place wrote to me to ask what I had in mind. I just like the name. It is an old whaling town, I believe. In any case, it has a completely Yankee sound" (Houghton Library, Harvard University).
66. The detail of their thinness will better be understood if we recall these lines from "The Revolutionists Stop for Orangeade":

    Ask us not to sing standing in the sun,
    Hairy-backed and hump-armed,
    Flat-ribbed and big-bagged.
    There is no pith in music
    Except in something false.

    (*CP,* pp. 102–3.)
67. That the glass coach *is* symbolic of the artist's vision of the world seems fairly apparent. This glass, like that of "Le Monocle de mon Oncle," allows the poet to perceive the world, but only through an intermediary element. The allusion to Cinderella's coach requires no gloss.
68. Kermode, *Romantic Image,* p. 14. The original passage refers to "the rarity and brevity" of those moments; but for Stevens, a poet of more fecund imagination than Arnold, the moments were not rare.
69. *NA,* p. 77.
70. *CP,* p. 19.
71. For a somewhat different reading of the poem, see Robert Pack, *Wallace Stevens* (New Brunswick, 1958), pp. 170–74.
72. William Blake, *Jerusalem, Poetry and Prose of William Blake,* ed. Geoffrey Keynes (London and New York, 1948), p. 436.

NOTES TO CHAPTER VI

1. "The Comedian as the Letter C," *CP*, p. 31.
2. Letter dated October 28, 1922, Wallace Stevens Manuscripts, Harriet Monroe Modern Poetry Library, University of Chicago.
3. Letter dated September 23, 1922, *ibid.*
4. *Ibid.*
5. In a letter to me, dated November 3, 1959.
6. The "Letter C" of the title suggests the incomplete nature of Crispin's voyage. His life is not over at the close of the poem; thus the circle remains unclosed. Further, as Hi Simons suggested, "After all his adventures, the condign but scarcely noble quotidian in which he ended was much like that from which he had started in Bordeaux. 'A nice shady home and daughters with curls.' Gelatines and jupes again. The same honest quilts. Same simple saladbeds." (" 'The Comedian as the Letter C': Its Sense and Its Significance," *Southern Review*, V [Winter 1940], 467.) The characteristic of ending at a point close to one's beginning is of course common to both Crispin and the letter C. The letter C is also one of the means by which Stevens enforced the parallels between Crispin and Candide, who is alluded to directly in the poem (*CP*, p. 42), and whose progress from naive heroic optimism to conservative realism sets the pattern for Crispin's progress. Finally, the letter C provided Stevens with one of the technical motifs that helped to organize the poem. In a letter to Renato Poggioli dated June 3, 1953, Stevens wrote: "It may sound a little difficult to translate *The Comedian as the Letter C*. The sounds of the letter C, both hard and soft, include other letters like K, X, etc. . . . However, it is true that the poem has made its way without reference to the sounds of the letter C." (Wallace Stevens Manuscripts, Houghton Library, Harvard University.)
7. "The Comedian as the Letter C," *CP*, p. 30.
8. Letter dated June 3, 1953, Wallace Stevens Manuscripts, Houghton Library, Harvard University.

9. *Wallace Stevens*, p. 45.
10. "The Comedian as the Letter C," *CP*, p. 41. If Kermode exaggerates the obscurity of *The Comedian*, Henry W. Wells, on p. 16 in his recent *Introduction to Wallace Stevens* (Bloomington, 1964), plunges recklessly to the opposite extreme when he remarks: "The early and brilliant 'Comedian as the Letter C' is, unlike most of its author's works, graced with a straightforward narrative so that it is less in need of explanatory comment. True, its highly rhetorical or ornamental style occasionally leads Stevens into something of a snarl. But these few darkened passages hardly demand special comment here." Wells's appraisal of the poem is hardly clarified when a moment later he says that " 'The Comedian as the Letter C' differs from most of Stevens' in that it seems clearer than it is. . . ."
11. *Ibid.*, pp. 40–41. It is interesting to note that Stevens, a member of a poetic generation fond of representing reality through such symbols as rusty springs in rusty lots, was always more inclined to use fruit for this same purpose. Besides plums, one thinks offhand of significant treatments in the *Collected Poems* of such fruit as oranges, watermelons, peaches, grapes, pineapples, apples, and bananas.
12. "The Comedian," *CP*, p. 42.
13. *Ibid.*, p. 41. The tom-tom allusion was to reoccur, fifteen years later, in the twelfth section of "The Man with the Blue Guitar," a poem which on a number of grounds may be considered a continuation of "The Comedian."
14. "The Comedian," *CP*, p. 27.
15. *Ibid.*, p. 28.
16. Hi Simons, *op cit.*, p. 455.
17. *CP*, p. 10.
18. "The Comedian," *CP*, p. 30.
19. Simons, *op. cit.*, p. 454.
20. *CP*, pp. 128–30.
21. "The Comedian," *CP*, p. 29.
22. *Ibid.*, p. 31. Cf. Stevens' observation in "The Noble Rider and the Sound of Words" that reality "is a jungle in itself."

(*NA*, p. 26). Some interesting parallels to Stevens' fascination with and ideas about "tropical reality" may be found in Aldous Huxley's essay on "Wordsworth in the Tropics," in the volume *Do What You Will* (New York, 1928), pp. 123–39. E. M. Forster draws a similar antithesis between barbaric and "civilized" nature in *A Passage to India*, where the shapelessness of the Indian landscape becomes a symbol of contemporary reality, as against the tidiness of the Grasmere countryside, associated with Wordsworth and traditional harmonies between man and his environment which can no longer be maintained.

23. "The Comedian," *CP*, p. 31. Yucatan itself symbolizes the "dead romantic," the escapist reaction to "meaningless" reality in which Crispin can no longer indulge.

24. *NA*, p. 138.

25. "The Comedian," *CP*, p. 30.

26. *Ibid.*, p. 32.

27. *Ibid.*, p. 33. It is possible that the thunder, like the hanged lover in *Three Travelers Watch a Sunrise (OP,* p. 132) serves to remind Crispin of the poverty and wretchedness, suffering and pity, without which poetry has neither love nor wisdom.

28. *Ibid.*, p. 34.

29. *Ibid.* Cf. Stevens' remark in a letter to Harriet Monroe dated October 28, 1922: "Often I have to let go, in the most insignificant poem, which scarcely serves to remind me of it, the most skyey of skyey sheets. And often when I have a real fury for indulgence I must stint myself." (Wallace Stevens Manuscripts, Harriet Monroe Modern Poetry Library, University of Chicago.) The "skyey sheets" of the letter occur also in "The Comedian," *CP*, p. 40.

30. "The Comedian," *CP*, p. 34. In connection with the allusion to Peking, some future student of Stevens' road to Xanadu may be interested in the fact that Miss Monroe's sister was in that city at this time, and occasionally sent to Stevens packages of tea and objets d'art that he had requested.

31. *Ibid.*, p. 35.

32. *Ibid.*, p. 37.
33. *Ibid.*, p. 39.
34. "A Short View of Wallace Stevens," *Life and Letters To-day*, XXVI (September 1940), 217. The gravamen of Symons' general charge against Stevens is that his work is "flippant" and contains no "objective view of life. . . ."
35. "The Poetry of Wallace Stevens," *Poetry*, LXXV (December 1949), 149–65.
36. *The Continuity of American Poetry* (Princeton, 1961), p. 387.
37. *Ibid.*
38. "The Comedian," *CP*, p. 37.
39. *Op. cit.*, p. 466.
40. "The Comedian," *CP*, p. 43.
41. Letter dated June 3, 1953, Wallace Stevens Manuscripts, Houghton Library, Harvard University.
42. Cf. my discussion of this point in Chapter II.
43. For Romantic theories of the poem as heterocosmic analogue, cf. M. H. Abrams, *The Mirror and the Lamp* (New York, 1958), *passim.*
44. *NA*, p. 17.
45. *Ibid.*, p. 78.
46. "The Comedian," *CP*, p. 39.

Works Cited

Abrams, M. H. *The Mirror and the Lamp: Romantic Theory and the Critical Tradition.* New York, 1958.

Aiken, Conrad. Letter to the author, dated September 9, 1960.

Benamou, Michel. "Le Thème du Héros dan la Poésie de Wallace Stevens," *Études Anglaises,* XII (1959), 222–30.

Bewley, Marius. "The Poetry of Wallace Stevens," *Partisan Review,* XVI (September 1949), 895–915.

Blackmur, R. P. *Language as Gesture: Essays in Poetry.* New York, 1952.

Blake, William. *Poetry and Prose,* ed. Geoffrey Keynes. London, 1948.

Boswell, James. *The Life of Dr. Johnson,* ed. R. W. Chapman. London, 1957.

Brown, Ashley and Robert S. Haller, eds. *The Achievement of Wallace Stevens.* Philadelphia, 1962.

Brown, Norman. *Life Against Death.* New York, 1959.

Bryer, Jackson R. and Joseph N. Riddel. "A Checklist of Stevens Criticism," *Twentieth Century Literature,* VIII, Nos. 3–4 (October 1962–January 1963), 124–42.

Burnshaw, Stanley. Letter to the author, dated October 5, 1961.

———. "Turmoil in the Middle Ground," *New Masses,* XVII (October 1, 1935), 41–43.

Works Cited

———. "Wallace Stevens and the Statue," *Sewanee Review*, LXIX (Summer 1961), 355–66.

Buttell, Robert. "Wallace Stevens at Harvard: Some Origins of His Theme and Style," *ELH*, XXIX (March 1962), 90–119.

Camus, Albert. *Neither Victims nor Executioners*. New York, 1960.

Caruth, Hayden. "Poets without Prophecy," *The Nation*, CXCVI (April 27, 1963), 354–57.

Cunningham, J. V. "The Poetry of Wallace Stevens," *Poetry*, LXXV (December 1949), 149–65.

Doggett, Frank. "Wallace Stevens' Later Poetry," *ELH*, XXV (June 1958), 137–54.

Finch, John. "North and South in Stevens' America," *Harvard Advocate*, CXXVII (December 1940), 23–26.

Fletcher, John Gould. "The Revival of Aestheticism," *The Freeman*, VIII (December 19, 1923), 355–56.

Ford, Charles Henri. "Verlaine in Hartford: Has the Mystery Man of Modern Poetry Really Another Self?" *View*, I (September 1940), 1, 6.

Frankenberg, Lloyd. *Pleasure Dome*. Cambridge, Mass., 1949.

Frye, Northrop. "The Realistic Oriole: A Study of Wallace Stevens," *Hudson Review*, X (Autumn 1957), 353–70.

Harstock, Mildred E. "Stevens' 'Bantams in Pine Woods,'" *The Explicator*, XVIII (March 1960), Item 33.

Harvard Advocate, CXXVII (December 1940), Wallace Stevens Issue; contains articles and remarks by F. O. Matthiessen, Marianne Moore, Allen Tate, William Carlos Williams, and others.

Howe, Irving. "Another Way of Looking at the Blackbird," *New Republic*, CXXXVII (November 4, 1957), 16–19.

Huxley, Aldous. *Do What You Will*. New York, 1928.

Jarrell, Randall. *Poetry and the Age*. New York, 1953.

Keats, John. *Letters*, ed. Maurice Buxton Forman. London, 1935.

Kenner, Hugh. *The Invisible Poet*. New York, 1959.

Kermode, Frank. *Puzzles and Epiphanies*, with an Introduction by William Phillips. New York, 1962.

———. *Romantic Image*. London, 1961.

———. *Wallace Stevens*. Edinburgh and London, 1960.

———. "The Words of the World: On Wallace Stevens," *Encounter*, XIV (April 1960), 45–50.

Kreymborg, Alfred. *A History of American Poetry: Our Singing Strength*. New York, 1934.

———. *Troubadour: An Autobiography*. New York, 1925.

Lafferty, Michael. "Wallace Stevens: A Man of Two Worlds," *Historical Review of Berks County*, XXIV (Fall 1959), 109–13, 130–32.

Laughlin, James, ed. *New Directions in Prose and Poetry*. New York, 1936.

"The Laureate of Hartford," *Business Week* (April 8, 1950), p. 94.

Lawrence, D. H. *Letters*, ed. Aldous Huxley. New York, 1932.

Lewis, Wyndham. *Time and Western Man*. Boston, 1957.

Loeb, Harold. *The Way It Was*. New York, 1959.

Lowell, Amy. *A Critical Fable*. Boston and New York, 1924.

Martz, Louis L. "Wallace Stevens: The World as Meditation," *Literature and Belief, English Institute Essays, 1957*, ed. M. H. Abrams. New York, 1958, pp. 139–65.

———. "The World of Wallace Stevens," *Modern American Poetry: Focus V*, ed. B. Rajan. London, 1950, 94–109.

Matthiessen, F. O. "Statement," *Harvard Advocate*," CXXVII (December 1940), 31.

Michelson, Max. Letter in "The Reader Critic," *The Little Review*, V (July 1918), 6.

Mitchell, Roger S. "Wallace Stevens: A Checklist of Criticism," *Bulletin of Biography*, XXIII, Nos. 9–10 (September–December 1962–January–April 1963), 208–11, 232–33.

Moore, Marianne. "Well Moused, Lion," *Dial*, LXXVI (January 1924), 84–91.

Morse, Samuel French. Letter to the author, dated November 3, 1959.

———. "The Native Element," *Kenyon Review*, XX (Summer 1958), 446–65.

———, ed. *Opus Posthumous*. New York, 1957.

Works Cited

——, ed. *Poems by Wallace Stevens*. New York, 1959.

——. *Wallace Stevens: A Preliminary Checklist of His Published Writings: 1898–1954*. New Haven, Conn., 1954.

——. *Wallace Stevens Checklist and Bibliography of Stevens Criticism*. Denver, Colorado, 1963.

Munson, Gorham B. "The Dandyism of Wallace Stevens," *Dial* LXXIX (November 1925), 413–17.

Nichols, Lewis. "A Talk with Mr. Stevens," *New York Times Book Review* (October 3, 1954), 3, 31.

O'Connor, William Van. *The Shaping Spirit: A Study of Wallace Stevens*. Chicago, 1950.

Pack, Robert. *Wallace Stevens: An Approach to His Poetry and Thought*. New Brunswick, New Jersey, 1958.

Peacock, Thomas Love. *The Four Ages of Poetry, etc.*, ed. H. F. B. Brett-Smith. Oxford, 1952.

Pearce, Roy Harvey. *The Continuity of American Poetry*. Princeton, 1961.

——. "Wallace Stevens: The Life of the Imagination," *PMLA*, LXVI (September 1951), 561–82.

Pieper, Josef. *Leisure the Basis of Culture*, trans. Alexander Dru, with an Introduction by T. S. Eliot. London, 1952.

Powys, Llewelyn. "The Thirteenth Way," *Dial*, LXXVII (July 1924), 45–50.

Ramsey, Warren. *Jules Laforgue and the Ironic Inheritance*. New York, 1953.

Rosenfeld, Paul. *Men Seen*. New York, 1925.

Simons, Hi. " 'The Comedian as the Letter C': Its Sense and Significance," *Southern Review*, V (Winter 1940), 453–68.

——. "The Genre of Wallace Stevens," *Sewanee Review*, LIII (Autumn 1945), 566–79.

——. "The Humanism of Wallace Stevens," *Poetry*, LXI (November 1942), 448–52.

——. "The Vicissitudes of Reputation, 1914–1940," *Harvard Advocate*, CXXVII (December 1940), 8–10, 34–44.

Skeat, Walter W. *An Etymological Dictionary of the English Language*. Oxford, 1882.

Soule, George. "Public Verse," *New Republic*, VI (March 25, 1916), 222–23.

Stallknecht, Newton. "Absence in Reality: A Study in the Epistemology of the Blue Guitar," *Kenyon Review*, XXI (Fall 1959), 545–62.

Stevens, Wallace. *Collected Poems*. New York, 1954.

——. Louis Untermeyer Collection, Lilly Library, Indiana University. Holdings include six letters from Stevens to Untermeyer, one letter from Untermeyer to Stevens.

——. *The Necessary Angel: Essays on Reality and the Imagination*. New York, 1951.

——. *Opus Posthumous*, ed. and with an Introduction by Samuel French Morse. New York, 1957.

——. *Poems by Wallace Stevens*, ed. and with an Introduction by Samuel French Morse. New York, 1959.

——. The Ronald Lane Latimer Papers, Harriet Monroe Modern Poetry Library, University of Chicago. Holdings include several unpublished poems in manuscript, holograph copies of "To the One of Fictive Music" and "Peter Quince at the Clavier," galley proofs, corrected by Stevens, of "Owl's Clover," and eighty odd letters from Stevens to Latimer, covering the years 1934–38, the majority of them related to the publication of *Ideas of Order and Owl's Clover* by Latimer's Alcestis Press.

——. Wallace Stevens Manuscripts, Harriet Monroe Modern Poetry Library, University of Chicago. Holdings include fifty-five letters from Stevens to Harriet Monroe, covering the years 1914 to 1935; proof sheets and manuscript copies of a number of Stevens' poems that appeared in *Poetry*, including "Sunday Morning"; and manuscript copy and proof sheets of "Three Travelers Watch a Sunrise," with comments by Harriet Monroe and revisions by Stevens.

——. Wallace Stevens Manuscripts, Houghton Library, Harvard University. Holdings include three letters from Stevens to William Stanley Braithewaite (1921–22); one letter to Bancel La Farge (1917) concerning stage setting for a production of "Carlos Among the Candles"; twenty-seven personal letters from Stevens to his friend Philip S. May (1930–45); eleven letters from Stevens to Renato

Poggioli, and six letters from Poggioli to Stevens (1953), concerning the translations into Italian of Stevens' poems which Poggioli was at the time working on; two letters to J. L. Sweeney concerning an unauthorized English edition of Stevens' poems; three letters to Oscar Williams and one from Williams to Stevens (1944) concerning anthology selections from Stevens' work. The letters to Poggioli are of great importance; they contain remarks by Stevens on individual poems, as well as a lengthy exegesis of "The Man with the Blue Guitar." Some of Stevens' comments were printed in Poggioli's *Mattino Domenicale ed Altre Poesie,* published in 1954.

Symons, Julian. "A Short View of Wallace Stevens," *Life and Letters Today,* XXVI (September 1940), 215–24.

Thorp, Willard. *American Writing in the Twentieth Century.* Cambridge, Massachusetts, 1960.

Tindall, William York. *Wallace Stevens.* University of Minnesota Pamphlets on American Writers, No. 11. Minneapolis, 1961.

Van Vechten, Carl. Letter to the author, dated September 6, 1960.

"Vice President of Shapes," *Time,* LXVI (August 15, 1955), 12.

Warren, Robert Penn. *Selected Essays.* New York, 1958.

Wells, Henry W. *Introduction to Wallace Stevens.* Bloomington, Indiana, 1964.

Williams, William Carlos. *Kora in Hell.* Boston, 1920.

———. *Selected Letters.* New York, 1957.

———. "Statement," *Harvard Advocate,* CXXVII (December 1940), 32.

Wilson, Edmund. *Axel's Castle.* New York, 1931.

———. *The Shores of Light.* London, 1952.

Winters, Yvor. *In Defense of Reason.* New York, 1943.

Yeats, William Butler. *Collected Poems.* New York, 1952.

Index

Index

Index